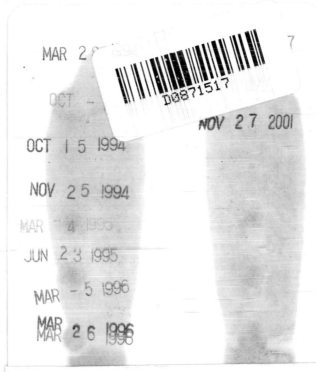

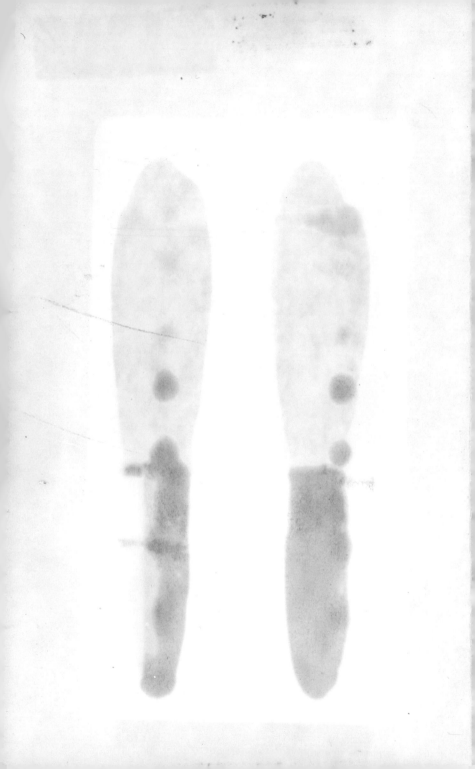

COME
BLOW
YOUR
HORN

CONNIE

Maybe I'll do a little modeling or become a secretary . . . or . . . a housewife.

ALAN

What?

CONNIE

Housewife. You know, sleep-in maids.

(Act I)

COME
BLOW
YOUR
HORN

A Comedy By

Neil Simon

Doubleday & Company, Inc.
Garden City, New York,
1963

All of the characters in this book are fictitious, and any resemblance to actual persons, living or dead, is purely coincidental.

Library of Congress Catalog Card Number 63–7713
Copyright © 1961 by Neil Simon
All Rights Reserved
Printed in the United States of America

CAST

(*In Order of Appearance*)

ALAN BAKER	Hal March
PEGGY EVANS	Arlene Golonka
BUDDY BAKER	Warren Berlinger
MR. BAKER	Lou Jacobi
CONNIE DAYTON	Sarah Marshall
MRS. BAKER	Pert Kelton
A VISITOR	Carolyn Brenner

TIME: The present.
PLACE: Alan's apartment in the East Sixties,
New York City.

ACT I: Six o'clock in the evening, early fall.

ACT II: Immediately after.

ACT III: Late afternoon. Three weeks later.

COME
BLOW
YOUR
HORN

ACT I

AT RISE: ALAN BAKER, *in a short Italian suede ski jacket is standing in the doorway being his charming, persuasive best in attempting to lure* PEGGY EVANS *into his bachelor apartment.* PEGGY *is in a ski outfit that fits her so snugly it leaves little room for skiing.* ALAN *puts down his valise, then slides* PEGGY'S *overnight bag out of her hand without her even noticing it and places it on the floor.* ALAN *is very adept at this game. Being good-looking, bright, thirty-three and single against* PEGGY'S *twenty-two years of blissful ignorance and eagerness to please, it appears that* ALAN *has all the marbles stacked on his side.*

PEGGY

Alan, no!

ALAN

Come on, honey.

PEGGY

Alan, no.

ALAN

(Taking off her ski jacket)

Just five more minutes. Come on.

PEGGY

Alan, no. Please.

(He pulls her into the living room)

ALAN

But you said you were cold.

PEGGY

I am.

ALAN

(Embracing her)

I'll start a fire. I'll have your blood going up and down in no time.

PEGGY

Alan, I want to go upstairs and take a bath. I've got about an inch of the New York Thruway on me.

ALAN

Honey, you can't go yet. We've got to have one last drink. To cap the perfect weekend.

PEGGY

It was four days.

ALAN

It's not polite to count . . . Don't you ever get tired of looking sensational?

PEGGY

Do you think I do?

ALAN

You saw what happened at the ski jump. They were looking at you and jumping into the parking lot . . . Come here.

(*He bites her on the neck*)

PEGGY

Why do you always do that?

ALAN

Do what?

PEGGY

Bite me on the neck.

ALAN

What's the matter? You don't think I'm a vampire, do you?

PEGGY

Gee, I never thought of that.

ALAN

If it'll make you feel safer, I'll chew on your ear lobe.

(*He does*)

PEGGY

(*Giggles*)

Kiss me.

ALAN

I'm not through with the hors d'oeuvres yet.

(*He kisses her*)

PEGGY

(*Sighs and sits on sofa*)
Now I feel warm again.

ALAN

Good.

PEGGY

Thank you for the weekend, Alan. I had a wonderful time.

ALAN

Yeah, it was fun.
(*Crossing toward bar*)

PEGGY

Even though he didn't show up.

ALAN

(*Stops and turns*)
Who?

PEGGY

Your friend from M-G-M.

ALAN

(*Continuing to bar. Quickly*)
Oh, Mr. Manheim. Yeah . . . Well, that's show biz.

PEGGY

Did it say when he expects to be in New York again?

ALAN

Did what?
(*Picks up carton containing scotch bottle*)

PEGGY

The telegram. From Hollywood.

ALAN

Oh! Didn't I tell you? Next week. Early part.

PEGGY

It's kind of funny now that you think of it, isn't it?

ALAN

What is?

PEGGY

Him wanting to meet me in a hotel.

ALAN

(*Taking bottle out of carton*)

It was a ski lodge.

PEGGY

Was it? Anyway, it was nice. I've never been to New Hampshire before.

ALAN

It was Vermont.

(*Putting down carton*)

PEGGY

Oh. I'm terrible with names. I can't imagine why an important man like that wants to travel all the way up there just to meet me.

ALAN

(*Puts bottle back on bar*)

I explained all that. Since this picture he's planning is all about a winter carnival, he figured the best place to meet you would be against the natural setting of the picture. To see how you photograph against the snow. That makes sense . . .

(*Not too sure*)

Doesn't it?

(*Crosses right*)

PEGGY

Oh, sure.

ALAN

Sure.

(*Pulls* PEGGY *up from couch and embraces her*)

PEGGY

We ought to go again sometime when it's not for business. Just for fun.

ALAN

That should be a weekend.

PEGGY

Maybe next time I could learn to ski.

ALAN

I wouldn't be surprised.

PEGGY

It's a shame we were cooped up in the room so long.

ALAN

Yes. Well, I explained, we had that bad break in the weather.

PEGGY

You mean all that snow.

ALAN

Exactly . . . But you make the cutest little Saint Bernard . . .
  (*He is just about to kiss her when the buzzer rings*)

PEGGY

That's the lobby.

ALAN

I don't hear a thing.

PEGGY

Maybe it's for me.

ALAN

My buzzer? You live up in the penthouse.

PEGGY

I know. But I'm always here.
  (*He looks at her quizzically, then goes to wall phone and picks it up*)

ALAN
  (*Into phone*)
Yes? . . . Who? . . . Buddy? . . . Hi, kid . . . Now? . . .
Well, sure. Sure, if it's important. You know the apartment.
  (*He hangs up*)
My kid brother.

PEGGY

Oh. I'd better go.

ALAN
  (ALAN *reaches for her again*)
This is the seventh floor. We still have over a minute.

PEGGY
  (*Eluding him*)
I want to go up and change anyway.

(She picks up her parka and goes to him, then says invitingly)

You think he'll be here long?

ALAN

Not when you ask me like that.

PEGGY

Why don't you come up in twenty minutes?

ALAN

Why don't you come down in nineteen?

PEGGY

All right. 'By, Alan.

ALAN

'By, Connie.

PEGGY

Peggy!

(She breaks from him)

ALAN

What?

PEGGY

Peggy! That's the third time this weekend you called me Connie.

ALAN

I didn't say Connie. I said Honey!

PEGGY

Oh!

ALAN

Oh!

PEGGY

Sorry.

(ALAN opens door)

(She smiles and exits)

(ALAN breathes a sigh of relief. Picks up suitcase and goes into bedroom as the doorbell rings)

ALAN

(Off stage)

Come on in, it's open.

(BUDDY BAKER, *his younger brother, enters with a valise in hand. Buddy is the complete opposite of Alan. Reserved, unsure, shy*)

BUDDY

Hello, Alan . . . Are you busy?
   (*Enters apartment and looks around*)

ALAN

(*Off stage*)
No, no. Come on in, kid.
   (ALAN *on*)
What's up?
   (ALAN *sees suitcase*)
What's in there?

BUDDY

Pajamas, toothbrush, the works.

ALAN

You're kidding.

BUDDY

Nope.

ALAN

You mean you left?
   (BUDDY *nods*)
Permanently?

BUDDY

I took eight pairs of socks. For me, that's permanently.

ALAN

I don't believe it. You can't tell me you actually ran away from home.

BUDDY

Well, I cheated a little. I took a taxi.
   (*Takes off coat and places it on suitcase*)

ALAN

You're serious. You mean my baby brother finally broke out of prison?

BUDDY

We planned it long enough, didn't we?

ALAN

Yes, but every time I brought it up you said you weren't
ready. Why didn't you say something to me?

BUDDY

When? You weren't at work since Thursday.

ALAN

Hey, did Dad say anything? About my being gone?

BUDDY

Not at the office. But at home he's been slamming doors. The
chandelier in the foyer fell down. Where were you?

ALAN

Vermont.

BUDDY

Skiing?

ALAN

Only during the day.

(*Sits on sofa and lights cigarette*)

BUDDY

I don't know how you do it. If I'm at work one minute after
nine, he docks my pay . . . and I get less to eat at home.

ALAN

Because he expects it from you. From me he says he expects
nothing, so that's what I give him.

BUDDY

You're better off. At least you're not treated like a baby. You
can talk with him.

ALAN

We don't talk. We have heart to heart threatening . . .

BUDDY

That's better than the subtle treatment I get. Last night I
came home three o'clock in the morning. He didn't approve.
What do you think he did?

(ALAN *shakes his head*)

As I passed his bedroom door, he crowed like a rooster. Cock-a-
doodle-doo.

ALAN

You're kidding. What'd you say?

BUDDY

Nothing. I wanted to cluck back like a chicken but I didn't have the nerve.

ALAN

Oh, he's beautiful.

BUDDY

And then yesterday was my birthday.
   (*Sits on sofa*)
Twenty-one years old.

ALAN

Oh, that's right. Gee, I'm sorry I wasn't there, Buddy. Happy birthday, kid.
   (*He shakes* BUDDY's *hand warmly*)

BUDDY

Thanks.

ALAN

I even forgot to get you a present.

BUDDY

I got one. A beaut. From Mom and Dad.

ALAN

What was it?

BUDDY

A surprise party. Mom, Dad, and the Klingers.

ALAN

Who are the Klingers?

BUDDY

Oh, the Klingers are that lovely couple the folks met last summer at Lake Mahopac.

ALAN

Why? They're not your friends.

BUDDY

Think. Why would they have the Klingers to meet me?

ALAN

They've got a daughter.

BUDDY

Oh, have they got a daughter.

ALAN

You mean they brought her with them?

BUDDY

In a crate.

ALAN

Let me guess. Naomi?

BUDDY

Close. Renee.

ALAN

Not much on looks but brilliant.

BUDDY

A genius. An I.Q. of 170. Same as her weight.

ALAN

And of course they had her dressed for the kill. They figured what she couldn't do, maybe Bergdorf could.

BUDDY

Nothing could help. So I spent the night of my twenty-first birthday watching a girl devour an entire bowl of cashew nuts.

ALAN

Oh, I'm sorry, kid.

BUDDY

(Rises, crosses right center)

It's been getting worse and worse. He looks in my closets, my drawers. He listens to my phone calls. I don't know what it is I've done, Alan, but I swear he's going to turn me in.

ALAN

Well, it's simple enough. He's afraid you're going to follow in my footsteps.

BUDDY

I did. I thought it over all day and realized I had to leave . . . Well—here I am.

ALAN

Oh, I'm so proud of you, Buddy. If you weren't twenty-one, I'd kiss you.

BUDDY

You really think I did the right thing?

ALAN

What did you do, rob a bank? You're only going to be living four subway stations away. You're still working for him, *aren't you?*

BUDDY

Well, there's going to be trouble there too.

ALAN

What do you mean?

BUDDY

I know I'm going to be struck by lightning for saying this . . . but I'm thinking of leaving the business.

ALAN

. . . On the level?

BUDDY

I'm not happy there, Alan. I'm not like you. You're good in the business . . . I'm not.

ALAN

It's just that you're inexperienced.

BUDDY

It's not only that. It just doesn't interest me. Gee whiz, there's a million more important things going on in the world today. New countries are being born. They're getting ready to send men to the moon. I just can't get excited about making wax fruit.

ALAN

Why not? It's a business like anything else.

BUDDY

It's different for you, Alan. You're hardly ever there.

(*He sits*)

You're the salesman, you're outside all day. Meeting people. Human beings. But I'm inside looking at petrified apples and pears and plums. They never rot, they never turn brown, they never grow old . . . It's like the fruit version of *The Picture of Dorian Gray*.

ALAN

(Follows)

You know why you feel that way? Because you never get a
chance to take the chains off. During the day it's all right.
But at night you've got to bite into the *real* fruit of life, Buddy,
not wax.

BUDDY

Yeah, I guess so.

ALAN

But that's all behind you now, right?

BUDDY

(Crosses downstage left)

Well . . .

(He looks at his watch)

In a few minutes anyway.

ALAN

(Crosses downstage left)

What do you mean?

BUDDY

Dad should be coming home soon.

ALAN

You mean you didn't tell him you were leaving?

BUDDY

I couldn't, Alan.

ALAN

Why not? Were you scared?

BUDDY

You bet I was. With you out of work these last few days he
hasn't been all smiles . . . And besides . . . I just didn't want
to hurt him . . . Sure he's stubborn and old-fashioned . . .
but he means well.

ALAN

I know, kid. I understand.

BUDDY

I left him at the plant and came home early tonight. Then I
wrote him a long letter explaining how I felt and left it on

his bed. And in the morning, I think I'll be able to reason with him. Don't you?

(*Crosses to* ALAN *right*)

ALAN

Frankly no, but what's the difference? I'm proud of you. You walked out of Egypt, kid. How about a drink? To celebrate. Scotch or bourbon?

(*He crosses to bar*)

BUDDY

(*Sits on sofa*)

Sure . . .

ALAN

Scotch, bourbon?

BUDDY

Scotch.

ALAN

Scotch it is.

BUDDY

And ginger ale.

ALAN

(*Stops*)

Scotch and ginger ale? . . . They must know you in every bar in town.

(*He makes drinks*)

Hey, how did Mom take all this?

BUDDY

(*Crosses and sits sofa*)

Oh, she's upset, of course. The most important thing to her is peace in the family.

ALAN

And a clean apartment.

BUDDY

(*Smiles*)

And a clean apartment.

ALAN

By the way, how is the Museum of Expensive Furniture?

BUDDY

Oh, the living room is still closed to the public!

ALAN

Living room? I don't remember ever seeing a living room.

BUDDY

Sure you did. The one that had the lamp shades wrapped in cellophane for the past twenty years.

ALAN

(*Placing drinks on coffee table*)

Oh, yes. I was outlawed from that room years ago for putting a cigarette in an ash tray.

BUDDY

. . . But you know why I really left home. I don't want to have milk and cake standing over the sink any more. I want to sit in a chair and eat like real people.

ALAN

Whoa, boy. You've got to start easy otherwise you'll get the bends. Maybe tonight you can hang your coat on the door-knob. Then maybe in a few days you'll be ready for bigger things . . . like leaving your socks on the floor.

BUDDY

(*Swings around right*)

Oh, it's going to be wonderful, just the two of us, Alan.

(*He looks around*)

Hey, I never realized it before, but this is a great apartment.

ALAN

Yeah. It comes a little high, but you pay for the atmosphere.

BUDDY

Oh, I almost forgot. How much is my rent?

ALAN

What rent?

BUDDY

For my share? I won't stay here unless I can pay my share.

ALAN

All right, sport. Give me thirty dollars.

BUDDY

Who are you kidding? This place is no sixty dollars a month.

ALAN

Look, that's your rent. Thirty dollars. When the old man starts paying you more, you can pay *me* more.

BUDDY

Well, just to start with. But we split everything else. The food and gas and electricity and everything. Agreed?

ALAN

(*Crosses right to* BUDDY, *bringing a drink*)

Agreed.

(*Hands* BUDDY *a drink*)

Here. You owe me seventy-five cents.

(*Raising his glass*)

Well, here's to the Baker Brothers. The dream we've planned for years . . . You take all the girls on the West Side, I'll take the East Side . . . and I'll get in trouble afore ye.

(*He winks affectionately at* BUDDY. BUDDY *drinks,* ALAN *watches*)

How is it?

BUDDY

(*Not very happy*)

Different.

ALAN

It should be. You just invented it.

(*The phone rings*)

Ten to one it's a gorgeous girl.

(*Phone rings again. He picks up phone*)

Hello? . . . Oh, Mom! . . . How are you, gorgeous? . . . We were just talking about you . . . Yes, about ten minutes ago . . . He's fine . . . Of course I'm going to take care of him . . . All right, sweetheart.

(*He holds phone out to* BUDDY)

It's the Curator of the Museum.

BUDDY

(*He takes the phone anxiously and sits sofa.* ALAN *goes to bar for refill*)

Hello, Mom? . . . How are you? . . . Fine . . . Fine . . .
No, no. I'll have dinner soon . . . I don't know, some place
in the neighborhood . . . Mom . . . Did Dad read the letter
yet? . . . Oh, still at the plant.

(ALAN *crosses to* BUDDY)

(BUDDY *breathes a little easier*)

What? . . . Mom, I don't want you to hide the letter . . . I
want him to read it . . . He what? . . . Oh, boy!

ALAN

What's wrong?

BUDDY

Well, I know that just makes it worse, Mom, but I can't—
Mom! . . . Mom! . . . Mom! . . .

ALAN

She's crying?
(*Nods*)

BUDDY

She's crying.

ALAN

Crying.

BUDDY

(*Back into phone*)

Mom, please calm down . . . No, Mom, that's not fair of you
to ask me that.

ALAN

What does she want you to do, come home?

BUDDY

(*Jumping up*)

Mom, don't tear up the letter. I can't come home.

ALAN

(*Crossing downstage left in front of table*)

Let me talk to her.

BUDDY

But what about my life?

ALAN

Let me talk to her.

BUDDY

Mom, please-don't-tear-up-the-letter!

ALAN

(Reaching for phone)

Give me the phone.

BUDDY

(Turns away)

Alan, will you wait a minute.

(Back into phone)

All right, Mom. Let me think about it. I will. I'll call you back . . . Later . . . I promise . . . All right . . . Don't tear up the letter . . . Good-by

(He hangs up)

ALAN

You'll think about what?

BUDDY

Dad called Mom about ten minutes ago from the plant. Screaming. Some customer is angry at you! Because you didn't show up for a meeting today?

ALAN

Oh, my gosh, Mr. Meltzer, I forgot.

BUDDY

Anyway, Mom's afraid when he finds out that I left on top of this he'll go to pieces.

ALAN

All right, all right. One thing has nothing to do with the other. I'll straighten him out.

BUDDY

But he's going to let this all out on Mom. And you know when he starts to yell. You could get killed just from the fall-out.

ALAN

Well, what do you want to do?

BUDDY

I don't know. Maybe I should go home.

(Picks up coat and suitcase)

ALAN

Go home? Why?

BUDDY

Why should Mother get the blame for something we've done?

ALAN

(*Follows*)

Don't ask me. I don't crow like a rooster at three o'clock in the morning.

BUDDY

What am I supposed to do?

ALAN

Grow up. Be a man. You're twenty-one years old.

(*Takes his suitcase and coat and puts them down by sofa*)

BUDDY

You mean just forget about it?

ALAN

Buddy, how long do you want to wait until you start enjoying life? When you're sixty-five you get social security, not girls.

BUDDY

I don't know how we got all twisted around. I'm on your side. I want to leave. It's Dad who's against it.

ALAN

Buddy, I know he means well. But he'll just never understand that things in life change. He's been in the wax-fruit business too long. *You've* changed.

BUDDY

I know, but—

ALAN

You're twenty-one years old now. You're ripe. Come on, kid. You've got one shoe off. Kick the other one off.

BUDDY

(*Looks at* ALAN *a moment, then shrugs*)

I—I guess you're right.

ALAN

Then you'll stay?

PEGGY

Now just relax . . . and try to forget about the picture business.
  (She massages)
No, I can feel it. You're still thinking about the studio.

BUDDY

No, I'm not. I swear I'm not.

(Act I)

BUDDY

(Nods)

Yeah . . . Why not?

ALAN

(Puts arm around him)

That's the kid brother I love and adore. Now go put your stuff in the bedroom.

BUDDY

You sure I won't be in your way here or anything?

(Picking up his coat and suitcase)

ALAN

Of course not. We just may have to work out a traffic system. I've got a girl coming down in a few minutes.

BUDDY

A girl? Why didn't you say so? Whenever you want to be alone, just say the word. I'll go out to a movie.

ALAN

Don't worry. With my schedule, you won't miss a picture this year.

(The doorbell rings)

You hear that? She's here ten minutes ahead of time.

(The doorbell rings again)

BUDDY

I'd better put this in here and go.

(Goes into bedroom)

ALAN

No, no. I want you to see her first.

(He crosses to door)

Ready for the thrill of your life?

(He opens the door a crack as he says:)

. . . and my third wish, O Geni, is that when I open the door, the most beautiful girl in the world will be standing there.

(He motions BUDDY *to come out of bedroom. As he opens the door, there stands his* FATHER, *scowling disgustedly)*

Dad!!

(BUDDY *enters and immediately goes back into bedroom closing door quietly behind him*)

FATHER

(*Steps in and looks at* ALAN *and nods disgustedly. He walks into the room.* ALAN *looks after him, dismayed, and seems puzzled when he doesn't see* BUDDY. *The* FATHER *examines the room. It is obvious he approves of nothing in the apartment*)

ALAN

(*Meeting him downstage center*)

Gee, Dad . . . this is a . . . pleasant . . . surprise.
   (*The* FATHER *looks at him as if to say, "I'll bet"*)
How . . . how are you?

FATHER

How am I? . . . I'll tell you sometime . . . That's how I am.
   (*He continues his inspection*)

ALAN

I've redecorated the place . . . How do you like it?

FATHER

Fancy . . . Very fancy . . . You must have some nice job.
   (*Sniffs highball glass*)

ALAN

I just got in, Dad. I was about to call you.

FATHER

The phone company shouldn't have to depend on your business.

ALAN

I wanted to explain what happened to me. Why I wasn't in the last two days.

FATHER

There's nothing to explain.

ALAN

Yes, there is, Dad.

FATHER

Why? I understand. You work very hard two days a week and you need a five-day weekend. That's normal.

ALAN

Dad, I'm not going to lie. I was up in Vermont skiing. I intended to be back Sunday night, but I twisted my bad ankle again. I couldn't drive. I thought it was broken.

FATHER

I'll send you a get-well card.

ALAN

I'm sorry, Dad. I really am.

FATHER

You're sorry. I can't ask more than that.

ALAN

I'll be in the office first thing in the morning.

FATHER

That's good news. You know the address, don't you?

ALAN

Yes, Dad. I know the address.

FATHER

See. I always said you were smart. So I'll see you in the morning.

ALAN

Right!

(ALAN *starts upstage*)

FATHER

(*Stops*)

Oh, by the way . . . How's the Meltzer account going?

ALAN

The Meltzer account?

(ALAN *comes back*)

FATHER

From Atlantic City? The one you bragged about was all wrapped up?

ALAN

Oh . . . er . . . fine.

FATHER

Fine? . . . I'm glad to hear that . . . Because he called today.

ALAN

(*Surprised*)

Oh? . . . About an order?

FATHER

Yes. About an order.

ALAN

(*A little skeptical*)

. . . Did . . . did we get one?

FATHER

Yes . . . We got one.

ALAN

. . . How much?

FATHER

How much?—guess.

ALAN

Well, Dad I—

FATHER

Guess! Guess how much we got from Meltzer.

ALAN

. . . Nothing?

FATHER

Bingo! Right on the button! . . . Bum!

ALAN

Dad, wait a minute . . .

FATHER

Did you have a nice weekend, bum? Do you know what it costs to go skiing for four days? Three thousand dollars a day? Bum!

ALAN

I tried to call him. I couldn't get a line through.

FATHER

On skis you tried to call him? You should be in the Olympics.

ALAN

(*Crossing to phone*)

I'll call him right back. I'll explain everything.

FATHER

Where you gonna call him?

ALAN

In Atlantic City.

FATHER

Who're you going to talk to? The Boardwalk? He's here!

ALAN

In New York?

FATHER

In the Hotel Croyden. For two days he's sitting waiting while you're playing in the snow.

ALAN

Dad, I promise you. I won't lose the account.

FATHER

Why? This would be the first one you ever lost? You want to see the list? You could ski (*gestures*) down your cancellations.

ALAN

I couldn't get back in time, Dad. Skiing had nothing to do with it.

FATHER

I'm sorry. I forgot. I left out golf and sailing and sleeping and drinking and women. You're terrific. If I was in the bum business I would want ten like you.

ALAN

That's not true. I put in plenty of time in the business.

FATHER

Two years. In six years you put in two years. I had my bookkeeper figure it out.

ALAN

Thank you.

FATHER

My own son. I get more help from my competitors.
  (*Starts to sit*)

ALAN

Well, why not? You treat me like one.

FATHER

(Jumping up)

I treat you? Do I wander in at eleven o'clock in the morning?
Do I take three hours for lunch . . . in night clubs? . . .
When are you there?

ALAN

What do you mean, when?

FATHER

When? When? You take off legal holidays, Jewish holidays,
Catholic holidays . . . Last year you took off Hallowe'en.

ALAN

I was sick.

FATHER

When you came back to work you were sick. When you were
sick you were dancing.

ALAN

In the first place, it's not true. And in the second place, what
good does it do coming in? You don't need me. You never ask
my advice about the business, do you?

FATHER

What does a skier know about wax fruit?

ALAN

You see? You see? You won't even listen.

FATHER

(He sits)

Come in early. I'll listen.

ALAN

I did. For three years. Only then I was "too young" to have
anything to say. And now that I've got my own apartment,
I'm too much of a "bum" to have anything to say. Admit it,
Dad. You don't give me the same respect you give the night
watchman.

FATHER

At least I know where he is at night.

ALAN

. . . You know where I am, too. Having fun. What's wrong
with it? I think what I do at night should be my business.

FATHER

Not when it's nighttime four days in a row. Listen, what do I care?

(*He rises and crosses right*)

Do whatever you want. Go ahead and live like a bum.

ALAN

Why am I a bum?

FATHER

Are you married?

ALAN

No.

FATHER

Then you're a bum!

ALAN

Give me a chance. I'll get married.

FATHER

I heard that for years. When you were twenty-six, twenty-seven, twenty-eight, even twenty-nine, you were a bachelor. But now you're over thirty and you're still not married, so you're a bum and that's all there is to it.

(*Turns away*)

ALAN

Who made thirty the closing date? All I want to do is have a little fun out of life like any other healthy, normal American boy.

FATHER

Healthy you are, American you are, normal you're not.

ALAN

What do you mean?

FATHER

Look at your brother, that's what I mean. That's normal. He'll be something, that kid. He'll never be like you. Not in a million years.

ALAN

Really? He might surprise you.

FATHER

That I'll bet my life on. He's in the plant the first thing in the morning, he puts in a whole day's work. No, that's one son I'll never have to worry about.

ALAN

Have you read your mail lately?

FATHER

What?

ALAN

Nothing.

FATHER

All right, I don't want to discuss anything more. I want to see you in the office tomorrow morning at eight o'clock.

ALAN

Eight o'clock? There's no one there then.

FATHER

You'll be there. And you'll be there two nights a week and Saturdays, holidays, birthdays, and vacations. I'm sick and tired of being the father. From now on I'm the boss.

ALAN

All right, Dad, but eight o'clock is silly. I have nothing to do until nine.

FATHER

(*Crossing up to foyer*)

You play solitaire all day anyway. You can get in three more games.

ALAN

Okay. Okay, I'll be there.

FATHER

With the Meltzer account. If you haven't got it signed and in your pocket . . . you can ski (*gesturing*) right into the unemployment office.

ALAN

I'll try, Dad. I'll really do my best.

FATHER

With your best, we're in trouble. From you I need a miracle.

(ALAN *sits downstage right center chair*)

Eight o'clock with the Meltzer account . . .

ALAN

Yes, Dad.

FATHER

The day your brother becomes like you, I throw myself in front of an airplane.

(*And with that he exits*)

(*As front door slams,* BUDDY *comes rushing out of the bedroom door in a state of shock*)

BUDDY

Did you hear that? I told you, Alan. I told you what he'd do.

ALAN

(*Crosses to phone*)

What hotel did he say, the Croyden?

BUDDY

Wait'll he reads that letter. He'll kill himself. He'll kill all of us. Like those stories in the Daily *News*. Alan, give me the phone.

(ALAN *dials 411*)

ALAN

Take it easy, will you. I've got to call Meltzer.

BUDDY

Meltzer? We've got to get to Mom before he gets home. She's got to tear up that letter.

ALAN

Will you relax. He's not going to kill anyone until he's had his supper . . . I'll straighten everything out.

BUDDY

How?

ALAN

All I've got to do is get Meltzer to sign.

(*Into phone*)

I'd like the number of the Hotel Croyden please.

BUDDY

Suppose you don't?

ALAN

There's no problem. He came to New York because I prom-
ised him a party . . .
   (*Into phone*)
What was that? Thank you.
   (*Dials number*)

BUDDY

I sure picked a rotten time to leave. It's going to be murder
up there.
   (*Starts to go*)
I'm going home.

ALAN

You walk out that door, I don't want you back.

BUDDY

   (*Coming back*)
Alan, why don't you help me?

ALAN

   (*Into phone*)
Mr. Martin Meltzer, please . . . Thank you.
   (*To* BUDDY)
I'm doing more than helping you. I'm saving you. It took you
two years to get this far. Next time it'll take you five.
   (*Into phone and rises*)
Hello? Mr. Meltzer? Hi? Alan Baker! . . . Where was I?
. . . I'm too embarrassed to tell you . . . You ready? . . .
Atlantic City . . . Yes. I thought you wanted me to come
there . . . I just didn't think . . . Sure, I had the girls with
me . . .

BUDDY

You're a lunatic!

ALAN

   (*Covers phone quickly*)
Will you shut up?
   (*Back into phone*)
What? . . . Well, can't you take the morning train back?

. . . Can I still get in touch with the girls? . . . They're here with me right now.

BUDDY

Where?

ALAN

(*Covers phone again quickly*)

I'll shove you in the closet.

(*Back into phone*)

What was that? . . . Yes . . . That was one of the girls you heard . . . Pretty?

(*He laughs. Turns head slightly from phone*)

Honey, he wants to know if you're pretty . . . Mr. Meltzer, did you ever see an ugly girl in the Copacabana line? . . . No, they're off this week . . . Yes, they're dying to . . . Your hotel. Room 326 . . . Half hour? You have the drinks ready, I'll bring the drinkers.

(*He laughs a phony laugh into the phone and hangs up*)

I hate myself.

(*He picks up book and thumbs through it quickly*)

BUDDY

I never saw anyone like you. Is it like this every night?

ALAN

Well, it's always slow before Christmas.

(*Reading from book*)

"Married . . . Married . . . Europe . . . Pregnant . . ."

(*Finds something in book*)

Ahhh, here we are. Chickie Parker.

(*He dials*)

BUDDY

Chickie Parker?

ALAN

And she looks just like she sounds.

(*Into phone*)

Hello? . . . Chickie? Don't you know you could be arrested for having such a sexy voice? . . . Alan . . . How could I? I just got in from Europe an hour ago . . . Switzerland . . . A specialist there told me if I don't see you within a half an hour, I'll die . . . Yes, tonight . . . A friend of mine is having a little party . . . Wonderful guy . . . Hundred laughs . . . Hey, Chickie, is your roommate free? The French girl? . . . Wonderful. Yes. Bring her . . . No, I can't. I've got to get the pretzels. Can you meet me there? The Hotel Croyden, Room 326, Marty Meltzer . . . A half hour . . . Marvelous. I just love you . . . What? . . . Yes, Alan *Baker.*

   (He hangs up)

Voila!

BUDDY

   (He's flabbergasted)

And it took me three months to get a date for my prom.

ALAN

I'd better get going.

   (He starts for bedroom when the buzzer rings. He stops)

Now what?

   (He crosses quickly to intercom and speaks into it)

. . . Hello? . . . Who?

   (Big surprise)

Connie!! . . . What are you doing here? . . . No, honey, no . . . Now? . . . Well, sure . . . sure, come on.

   (He hangs up)

Of all the nights.

BUDDY

Who's that?

ALAN

A girl.

BUDDY

Another one? Is she coming up?

   (ALAN nods)

ALAN

   (Half to himself)

She wasn't due back in town till tomorrow. What a time to show up.

BUDDY

Then why are you seeing her?

ALAN

Oh, I can't give this girl the brush.

BUDDY

I thought that part would be easy.

ALAN

You don't understand. This girl is different. She's not like . . . well, she's different.

BUDDY

You mean this one's for serious?

ALAN

Who said serious? I just said different.

BUDDY

Oh boy, would that solve everything at home if you got married. You know Mom's had an open line to the caterers for three years now.

ALAN

Married? Me? With all this? Are you crazy?

BUDDY

Well, I just thought—since she's a *nice* girl . . .

ALAN

She's the *nicest* . . . but I'm working on it . . . Listen, you'd better blow. I want to see her alone.

(*Doorbell rings*)

BUDDY

Okay.

(*He starts for the door*)

ALAN

Oh! Hey, go out the service entrance in the kitchen . . . Come back in a few minutes.

BUDDY

(*He nods and goes to kitchen door*)

Boy, no wonder you come in at eleven o'clock in the morning!

(*He exits*)

(ALAN *crosses quickly to the door and opens it about an*
inch and says aloud:)

ALAN

And my third wish, O Geni, is that when I open my eyes, the
most beautiful girl in the world will be standing there.

(*He opens door, turns and looks*)

(CONNIE *is standing there, holding an octagonal hat box*)

(ALAN *crossing downstage right*)

O Joy! My third wish has been granted. Enter, beautiful lady.

(CONNIE *enters*)

CONNIE

Well, I guess it's safe as long as you've used up the other two
wishes.

ALAN

How are you, Connie?

CONNIE

Fine . . . now that I'm back.

ALAN

(*He embraces her*)

Mmm. How does a girl get to smell like that?

CONNIE

She washes occasionally.

(*Holding package between them*)

ALAN

Come here. I've been thinking about this moment for two
whole weeks.

(*He tries to get closer*)

Will you put down that package.

CONNIE

(*She presents it to him*)

After you open it.

ALAN

(*He takes it*)

What is it?

CONNIE

A present.

ALAN

For me? Why?

CONNIE

(*She shrugs*)
I like you! . . . And I missed you.

ALAN

Well, I did too, but I didn't get you a present.

CONNIE

Well, don't get upset about it. I just like you six dollars and
ninety-eight cents more than you like me . . . Open it.
(*Unbuttons jacket*)

(*He opens it*)

ALAN

(*He looks in box. He is overwhelmed*)
Connie! . . . My ski hat!
(*He takes it out of box*)

CONNIE

It's like the one you lost, isn't it?

ALAN

(*He is really quite thrilled with it*)
It's the same thing.
(*He looks inside at the label*)
It's the identical one I bought in Switzerland. I've looked all
over New York for this. Where (*Puts box on fireplace chair*)
did you ever get it?

CONNIE

In Montreal . . . It wasn't hard. Up there the newsstand
dealers wear (*He puts hat on—She puts jacket on sofa*) them.

ALAN

It even fits. How did you know my head size?

CONNIE

I've got an imprint on my neck.

ALAN

(*Throws hat on sofa*)
Connie, you're wonderful. Only *you* would think of a thing
like this.

CONNIE

Well, I *thought* of a watch, but I could afford this better.

ALAN

Come here you.

(*He takes her in his arms*)

CONNIE

(*Coyly*)

Ah, the pay-off.

ALAN

Thank you very much.

(*He kisses her*)

CONNIE

You're welcome—very much.

(ALAN *moves to embrace her. She backs away*)

CONNIE

Alan relax.

ALAN

I'm not through yet.

(*She crosses left*)

CONNIE

I've just come eight hundred miles in a prehistoric train and I'm tired, hungry, and too weak to be chased around the sofa.

ALAN

(*Crosses to Connie*)

I'll carry you. We'll save lots of time and energy.

(*He moves after*)

CONNIE

Alan, please don't take advantage. I've got enough handicaps as it is.

ALAN

Like what?

CONNIE

(*Wilting*)

Like being on your side.

(*He grabs her and she swings around right of him*)

It isn't fair. You and me against me is not fair. What is it you've got?

ALAN

I don't know. Am I terribly good-looking?

CONNIE

Oh, God, no. You've got just enough things wrong with your face to make you very attractive . . . It's something else. Some strange power you have over me. But beware. The day I find out what it is, I'll have a gypsy destroy the spell with a dead chicken.

ALAN

You little fool. Nothing can stop the Phantom Lover.
    (*He starts after her*)

CONNIE

Alan, no!
    (*Backs right*)

ALAN

    (*Stalking her*)
One kiss. If it leaves you cold, I'll stop. But if it gets you all crazy, we play house rules.

CONNIE

    (*Moves so chair right is between them*)
Now, Alan, play fair.

ALAN

I'll keep my hands behind my back. I'll spot you a five-point lead. I'll only be permitted to use my upper lip.
    (*Steps up on chair*)

CONNIE

Alan, not now. Please. I haven't got the strength to put up an interesting fight. I just wanted to see you before I fell into bed for the next week and a half.

ALAN

Okay.
    (*He pecks her*)
A rough tour, heh?
    (*ALAN gets down off chair*)

CONNIE

This was the roughest.
    (*Sits on right arm of chair*)

ALAN

(*He laughs*)
You poor kid. When does the show go out again?

CONNIE

They leave in two weeks.

ALAN

They? . . . Not you?

CONNIE

(*Smiles*)
Not me.

ALAN

Why not?

CONNIE

I just suddenly decided to quit.

ALAN

Oh. Well, have you got another show lined up?

CONNIE

Well . . . it's not just the show I quit . . . It's show business.

ALAN

(*He looks at her*)
. . . Are you serious?

CONNIE

(*She nods. She doesn't want to make a big thing of it now*)
I'll tell you all about it tomorrow.
    (*Starts left*)
Will you call me, darling? . . . In the afternoon?

ALAN

Wait a minute. I want to hear about this.

CONNIE

There's nothing to tell.

ALAN

Nothing to tell? You're giving up your career and there's nothing to tell?

CONNIE

(*She laughs*)

Oh, Alan, darling . . . what career?

ALAN

What do you mean, what career? You're a singer, aren't you?

CONNIE

Well, I wouldn't invest in it.

ALAN

I don't get it. Things are going so well for you . . . All those musicals you do.

CONNIE

(*Sits sofa*)

They're not musicals. They're industrial shows. Two-hour commercials completely uninterrupted by entertainment.

ALAN

(*Sits sofa and puts hat on table behind sofa*)

I'm serious.

CONNIE

I'm dead serious. This past month we did a show for the Consolidated Meat Packers. Have you any idea what it's like singing "Why not take all of me"* dressed as a sausage?

ALAN

(*He smiles*)

It sounds funny.

CONNIE

Maybe to you. But I've seen butchers sit there and cry.

ALAN

All right, so it's not *My Fair Lady*. You don't expect it to come easy, do you?

CONNIE

I don't expect it to come at all. Not now. Alan . . .

(*Breaks left*)

---

* Line from "All of Me" by Seymour Simons and Gerald Marks. © Copyright 1931 Bourne, Inc., New York, N.Y. Copyright renewed. Used by permission.

I'd work my throat to the bone if I thought I had a chance . . .
or if I wanted it that much. But somehow lately I don't care
any more . . . I guess it started when I met you.

   (*Sits left arm*)

ALAN

Honey, everyone gets discouraged. But you don't suddenly
throw away a promising career.

CONNIE

Promising? Even you once said I was a lousy singer.

ALAN

No, I didn't. I said you had a lousy voice. There's a big difference.

CONNIE

There is?

ALAN

Of course. You've got looks, personality. That's all you need
in the music business today. Hockey players are making
albums.

CONNIE

It's *not* enough, Alan. You've got to have talent too.

ALAN

Only if you want to be good. Not if you want to be a star.

CONNIE

Well, it's pretty evident I'm not going to be either.

ALAN

I just don't understand your attitude.

CONNIE

I don't understand *yours*. The world isn't losing one of its great
artists.

ALAN

What suddenly brought all this on?

CONNIE

   (*Sits left of him*)

It's very simple. I just got tired of being away from you so long.

ALAN

   (*Withdrawing slightly*)

. . . Oh! . . . Well . . . if that's what you want.

Come Blow Your Horn

CONNIE

That's it. No more traveling. No more buses and trains and long-distance phone calls.

(She moves closer)

I don't want to be more than a thirty-five cent taxi ride away from you.

ALAN

(Getting a little jittery)

You . . . seem to have made up your mind.

CONNIE

Yes. And what a relief it is.

ALAN

Well . . . What will you do now?

CONNIE

I'll manage.

(ALAN rises—drifts right of center)

Girls are doing it every day. I'll maybe do a little modeling or become a secretary . . . or . . . a housewife.

ALAN

(Turns to face her)

What?

CONNIE

Housewife. You know . . . sleep-in maids.

ALAN

(Serious)

What do you mean?

CONNIE

It was a joke . . . You didn't get it.

ALAN

(Deadpan)

Yeah, I get it . . . It's funny.

(Looks at his watch)

Holy mackerel, look at the time.

(Starts upstage left)

Honey, I'm awfully sorry but I've got an important business appointment. Can I call you later?

CONNIE

No. I want to finish talking.

ALAN

About what?

CONNIE

Housewives.

ALAN

What about them?

CONNIE

You act as if you never heard of them.

ALAN

Sure I did. My mother's a housewife.

Connie, sweetheart . . . This is serious talk. Let's set aside a whole night for it. But right now I've really got to run.

   (*Holds her jacket out for her*)

CONNIE

How far?

ALAN

What?

CONNIE

I must have touched a nerve or something.

ALAN

That's not true. We've discussed marriage before, haven't we?

CONNIE

Yes. On this very couch. Or were they just campaign promises?

ALAN

What difference did it make? I didn't win the election, did I?

CONNIE

The returns aren't all in yet.

ALAN

   (*He looks at his watch nervously*)

Connie, honey. *You're* tired and I've got a business appointment *.* . .

   (*Holds jacket out again*)

CONNIE

At seven o'clock?

ALAN

It won't take long. I can be through by ten.

CONNIE

I'll bet you can.

ALAN

What do you mean?

CONNIE

Oh, Alan, I'm a big girl. You've got a date.

ALAN

It's a business appointment . . . And besides, I didn't expect you back until tomorrow.

CONNIE

You know, something just occurred to me.
    (*Rises*)
A few minutes ago I couldn't understand why you were fighting so hard to keep me in show business. It's suddenly very clear.

ALAN

What is?

CONNIE

It's not *my* career you're worried about. It's *yours!*

ALAN

My career??

CONNIE

As a lover.
    (*Grabs jacket and crosses right center*)
That's why you want me to stay out on the road.

ALAN

Why? I'm crazy about you.

CONNIE

Yes . . . when I'm here. The minute I leave . . . substitution. Oh, it's beautiful. A bachelor's dream. The two-platoon system.
    (*Putting on jacket*)

ALAN

What are you talking about?

CONNIE

You'll never grow stale, Alan. Or bored. Not as long as you keep rotating the crops every two weeks.

ALAN

You're not being fair.

(*Crossing downstage left*)

I never said I didn't want to get married. But you come in here and make it sound like an emergency.

CONNIE

For some strange reason I thought you felt the same as I did. These past six months were . . .

ALAN

They were wonderful. That's why I hate to see them end.

CONNIE

END! Getting married is the end?

ALAN

I didn't mean it that way. Connie, you've got to understand, in a way a thirty-three-year-old guy is a lot younger than a twenty-four-year-old girl. That is, he may not be ready for marriage yet.

CONNIE

Let's leave the third person out of this. You mean you.

ALAN

The point is, I didn't actually start my bachelor fling until late in life. And to tell the truth, I don't know if I'm flung out yet.

CONNIE

You would be if you were in love with me.

ALAN

I am. Very much in love . . . only . . . I don't know. I'm like a kid with a few chocolates left in the box. I want to finish them first.

CONNIE

Will you stop twisting thoughts. Now you're making it sound as if I'm taking candy from a baby.

(*Crosses right and sits*)

ALAN

Don't take my place in life.

BUDDY

How have I taken your place?

ALAN

I run the water for a bath and five minutes later I hear you splashing in there. You're using my barber, my restaurants, my ticket broker, my apartment, and my socks. How's it going, kid, am I having fun?

(Act III)

ALAN

No, I'm not. I'm leveling with you. Sure I see other girls. I'm only human but (*Crossing toward bar*) you must admit although these past six months were wonderful and exciting, I *have* made certain sacrifices that go against the very nature of man.

(*Turns to her*)
And you know from whence I speak.

CONNIE

The subject hasn't exactly been taboo.

ALAN

(*Crosses left*)
True it was discussed. But it never got off the drawing board. If it were another girl, I'd be in Tahiti painting by now. But here I am. Still battling it out.

CONNIE

The war would be over if I knew just what it was we were fighting for.

ALAN

I don't think I follow that.

CONNIE

All right, then, Alan, let's have the truth. Either you've said to yourself, "I'm going to marry this girl," or, "I'm going to have an affair with her." All I ask is that you let me in on your decision. If marriage is out just say so. I won't run. I'll stay and fight for my honor the way a girl who's been properly brought up should. And I can truthfully tell you I'll lose the battle before long, because, damn it, I'm in love with you. But if you're really in love with me, you've got to tell me and be prepared to back it up with the rest of your life.

(*Rises*)
Well, which is it going to be, Alan? Do we march down the aisle or into the bedroom?

ALAN

(*He stares at her unbelievingly a few seconds*)

That's the lousiest thing I ever heard . . . What am I supposed to say?

(*Starts right*)

CONNIE

Say what you really feel.

ALAN

You mean if I want to make love to you all I have to do is speak up?

CONNIE

Loud and clear.

ALAN

You're a nut.

(*Breaks left*)

A sweet, beautiful nut!

CONNIE

I'm waiting, Alan.

ALAN

(*Turning to her*)

For what? If I say I want you, you're mine. If I say I love you, I'm yours.

CONNIE

It's that simple.

ALAN

Well, I'm not going to play.

(*Crosses left*)

It's more dangerous than Russian roulette.

CONNIE

It's just being honest with each other, Alan. That's what you're afraid of. You won't even be honest with yourself.

ALAN

How can I be? I don't know what I want yet.

CONNIE

I didn't say you *had* to love me. I just want to know if you do.

ALAN

(*Crossing right to center*)

If I want you I don't have to love you, but if I love you I

shouldn't want you—I . . . I don't know. You've got to be an I.B.M. machine to figure out this affair.

CONNIE

I guess so. I forgot to make room for human failing.

ALAN

Boy oh boy, for an innocent little girl you sure play rough.

CONNIE

I didn't choose the game, Alan.
  (*She starts to go*)

ALAN

Where are you going?
  (*He stops her*)

CONNIE

I'd say you needed a chance to think.

ALAN

No, I don't.

CONNIE

You mean you've made up your mind?

ALAN

Yes . . . Yes, I've made up my mind.

CONNIE

. . . Well?

ALAN

You mean, no matter what I say, you'll go along with it?

CONNIE

To the letter.

ALAN

Okay . . . Okay, then . . . We march into the bedroom.

CONNIE

  (*Stares at him*)
That's the lousiest thing I ever heard.

ALAN

Uh huh. You see. You see. It's not so much fun when the *dentist* is sitting in the chair is it? You don't like it when I hold the drill.

CONNIE

I'm not complaining, Alan. I asked for it.

ALAN

Oh, that you did. And I called your little bluff, didn't I?

CONNIE

You certainly did.

(*She goes up to door*)

ALAN

Where are you going?

CONNIE

Back to my hotel.

ALAN

(*Crossing up left of her*)

All right, wait a second, Connie. The joke is over. You're embarrassed because I made you lose face. I'm sorry. But when you pushed me into a corner like that I had no choice.

CONNIE

Oh, my face is still all there, Alan. I just figure if I'm going into business here I might as well get the rest of my merchandise.

(*She goes blowing him a kiss.* ALAN *stares after her*)

ALAN

. . . No . . . Never happen . . . Not her . . .

(*The doorbell rings.* ALAN *rushes to it. He opens it expectantly. It's* BUDDY)

Oh, it's you.

BUDDY

Hey, was that her?

ALAN

Where'd you go?

BUDDY

Downstairs for a sandwich. Now that's what I call a pretty girl.

(ALAN *gets coat from closet*)

ALAN

You stay away from that kind. They're nothing but trouble.

BUDDY

How did it go?

ALAN

Oh, fine. Fine.

BUDDY

I thought maybe the other girl walked in.

ALAN

What other girl?

BUDDY

The one you were expecting. From upstairs. Didn't you call her?

ALAN

Peggy! O, my gosh, I forgot.
(*He crosses quickly to telephone. Throwing coat over sofa back*)

BUDDY

(*Crosses downstage right center*)
You ought to get one of those maps with the stick pins so you know where they are all the time.

ALAN

(*Dialing*)
I don't know what I'm doing tonight. What's that number again?

BUDDY

Is she as pretty as the one that just left?

ALAN

Peggy? Prettier. With none of the disadvantages.

BUDDY

Boy, what a great place to live. And all for thirty bucks a month.
(*Sits right center chair*)

ALAN

(*Hangs up*)
Hey, that's right. I forgot we're sharing everything. How would you like to meet her?

BUDDY

Who?

ALAN

Peggy. From upstairs.

BUDDY

(*Jumps up*)
Me? Are you kidding?

ALAN

Why? She's coming down anyway. No sense in sending her
home empty-handed.

BUDDY

But she's expecting you.

ALAN

Turn the lights down low. She won't figure it out till she's
going back up in the elevator.

BUDDY

You're crazy.

ALAN

No. That's how I met her. She rang the wrong bell one night.
There's some poor guy in this building waiting for her since
last July.

BUDDY

You're not serious, Alan. She probably baby-sits for boys like
me.

ALAN

No. She's only twenty-two.

BUDDY

I'm talking about experience, not age. I didn't realize it until
I got here tonight, but I've been living in a convent all my life.

ALAN

Buddy, trust me. She'll be crazy about you.

BUDDY

(*Crossing away left*)
No, she won't. I don't want to meet her, Alan.

ALAN

(*Crossing to him*)

I don't get you. Where's your spirit of adventure? You sound
like an old man.

ALAN

BUDDY

An old man?

ALAN

Sure, look at the way you dress. Why does a young boy like you
wear a black suit?

BUDDY

It's not black. It's charcoal gray.

ALAN

Whatever it is, you look like Herbert Hoover.

BUDDY

I'm sorry. I'll buy an all-white suit tomorrow.

ALAN

Buddy, I don't do this for everyone. Just brothers I love.

BUDDY

I'd like to, Alan, but gee, I had other plans.
   (*Break away left*)

ALAN

What other plans?

BUDDY

They've got that emergency UN meeting on television tonight I'd really like to see it.

ALAN

   (*Crossing to him*)
The UN? Buddy, if I offered this to the Security Council,
the meeting would be off tonight.

BUDDY

Look, maybe you're not interested in what's going on in the
world, but I am.

ALAN

I'm interested in what's going on with you. What is it? Are
you afraid?

BUDDY

Yes—I mean, **no.**

ALAN

You mean, yes.

BUDDY

No, I don't.

ALAN

You know, something just occurred to me. Is it possible that—

BUDDY

You're going to be late, Alan.

ALAN

I figured you were in the Army, overseas. Paris. I took it for granted—

BUDDY

(*Crosses up left of sofa*)

I got around.

ALAN

Where? In a sightseeing bus?

BUDDY

What are you making such a fuss about? What's so damn important about it, anyway?

ALAN

(*Crosses upstage right of sofa*)

It's plenty important.

BUDDY

(*Evades him crossing downstage right*)

I'll get around to it soon enough.

ALAN

Buddy, baby, why didn't you tell me?

(*Crosses right to* BUDDY)

That's what big brothers are for. This is the answer to your problem.

BUDDY

I haven't got a problem.

ALAN

You haven't, huh?

BUDDY

Look, there's a big difference between the way you and I operate. If I get a handshake from a girl I figure I had a good night.

ALAN

With Peggy, all you have to do is say "Hello." From there on it's downhill.

BUDDY

It can't be that easy. I know. I've tried.

ALAN

Look kid, I wanted to get you a birthday present anyway. Now I found something you haven't got.

BUDDY

I don't want it. I'm happy the way I am.

ALAN

Buddy, please. If not for your sake, then for mine.

BUDDY

For yours?

ALAN

Ever since I moved out, I felt I haven't really been looking after you . . . the way a big brother should. I want to make it up to you, kid.

BUDDY

I'm not complaining. You've been fine.

ALAN

It would really give me pleasure, Buddy, to do this for you . . . It's something a father could never do.

BUDDY

I'll say.

ALAN

But brothers, well, it's different Buddy . . . I feel that it's my duty and privilege to help you at this very important time of your life. What do you say, Buddy? . . . Please!

BUDDY

Well . . . if it'll make you happy, all right.

ALAN

Thanks, kid.

(BUDDY *shrugs.* ALAN *crosses to phone and dials—*BUDDY *crosses right*)

You'll see. This'll be set up so perfectly, you won't even have
to say a word to her . . .

   (*Hums "In a Little Spanish Town"*)

   (*Into phone*)
Hello? Peggy? . . . Yeah . . . No, no, wait a minute . . .

   (*He rises*)
I have good and bad news . . . First the bad news. I've got to
go out . . . No, most of the evening. Important business . . .
You ready for the good news? . . . He's here . . . Manheim!

                              BUDDY
Who?

                              ALAN
   (*Into phone*)
Oscar Manheim, the producer from M-G-M.

                              BUDDY
   (*Runs left of center*)
What?????

                              ALAN
Just as you left . . . He's staying in my apartment tonight . . .
He wants to meet you.

                              BUDDY
I gotta get out of here.

   (*He starts to go*)

                              ALAN
   (*Into phone*)
Yes, now . . . I told him all about you.

                              BUDDY
Please, Alan.

                              ALAN
   (*Into phone*)
Ten minutes? . . . Fine . . . Oh, don't dare thank me,
honey. I'm really doing *him* the favor.

   (*He hangs up*)
The ball's over the fence, kid. All you've got to do now is run
the bases.

BUDDY

Are you out of your mind? Me? A producer?

ALAN

You want to be a director? I'll call her back.
  (*Motions to phone*)

BUDDY

But why did you tell her that?

ALAN

Just to make it easier for you.

BUDDY

Easier?

ALAN

Now the pressure's off you. It's all on her.

BUDDY

What are you talking about?

ALAN

She's got a bug about getting into pictures. Now's her chance to prove how really talented she is.

BUDDY

How would I know?

ALAN

Because you're a big producer from M-G-M, Oscar Manheim.

BUDDY

Doesn't she know what he looks like?

ALAN

No. I made him up. Sounds real, huh?

BUDDY

Made it up? But she could call M-G-M and check.

ALAN

She doesn't know how to dial. Look. She's been auditioning for years without making a picture. She's got more money than M-G-M. She's having too much fun being discovered.

BUDDY

What am I supposed to do, make her a star?

ALAN

No. Just give her a small part in the picture.

BUDDY

What picture??

ALAN

I Was a Teen-age Producer. I don't know. Can't you make up
a picture?

BUDDY

  (*Breaking away right*)
No. Right now I can't even think of my own name.

ALAN

  (*Gets ready to leave*)
You're my brother. When the chips are down, you'll come
through.

BUDDY

A twenty-one-year-old movie producer. Holy cow!
  (*Crosses left to sofa*)

ALAN

Well, I'd better get going.

BUDDY

Wait a minute. When is she going to be here?

ALAN

Ten minutes. She just lives upstairs.

BUDDY

Ten minutes? I don't feel so good.

ALAN

Look, if you're really too scared I'll call her back and cancel it.

BUDDY

No. No, never mind.

ALAN

You won't admit it, but you're glad I called. Is there anything
you need?

BUDDY

Yeah. A drink.

ALAN

Here you are.
  (*Hands drink to him. Then picks up trench coat*)

BUDDY

Well, here's to Oscar Wilhelm.

ALAN

Manheim.

BUDDY

Oh, jeez.

(*He drinks it all quickly*)

ALAN

Hey, take it easy with that stuff.

(*Crossing up to foyer; puts on trench coat*)

BUDDY

Can you imagine if I drop dead and she calls the police.
They'll bury me in Hollywood.

ALAN

It's going to be the greatest night of your life. You'll thank me
for it some day.

(*He's at the door*)

BUDDY

Alan!

ALAN

Yes?

BUDDY

Will you call before you come home?

ALAN

I'll call, I'll ring the doorbell and I'll cough loud as soon as I'm
within two blocks of the house.

(*He opens the door*)

So long, kid. And happy birthday!

(*And he's gone*)

(BUDDY *stares after him a minute*)

BUDDY

Happy birthday! . . . Why couldn't he get me a tie like everyone else? . . . How'd I get talked into this?

(*He rubs his stomach as he apparently just got a twinge of
nervousness. He picks up both glasses and puts them on*

*bar. Starts right, gets a thought, looks at his own jacket.
Runs up to hall closet, takes out jacket, looks at it, puts it
back. Then he takes out a bright blue smoking jacket, runs
down to sofa, takes off his jacket, throws it on sofa, throws
hanger on sofa table and puts on smoking jacket. Picks up
cigarette holder from coffee table, inserts cigarette and starts
to light it. As he does so door bell rings. He stands para-
lyzed with fear. Screams)*

Oh! . . . Just a sec . . .

*(He looks around in a panic. He starts upstage, sees his
jacket on sofa and throws it under back of sofa. Then he
runs to the door and stops quickly to compose himself. He
straightens himself up. Hell, he's going to go through with
it. He opens the door. A small, rather harassed woman in
her late fifties stands there)*

(Yells)

Mom!

WOMAN

(Curtain falls as she speaks crossing downstage right)
Oh, darling, I'm so glad you're here.

BUDDY

(Follows—in a state of shock)
Mom! . . .

CURTAIN

ACT II

The same.

AT RISE: BUDDY *is franti-cally pacing back and forth. Buddy is about to have his first experience and here sits his mother.*

Mrs. BAKER *is a woman who has managed to find a little misery in the best of things. Sorrow and trouble are the only things that can make her happy. She was born in this country, dresses in fine fashion and in general her speech and appearance are definitely American. But she thinks Old World. Superstitions, beliefs, customs still cling to her. Or rather she clings to them. Because of this, we can't take her hysterics too seriously.*

BUDDY

Mom, are you feeling all right?

MOTHER

Darling, can I have a cold glass of water? I almost fainted on the subway.

BUDDY

Mom, what are you doing here?

MOTHER

I got such a dizzy spell. I never thought I'd get here.

BUDDY

Mom . . . what did you want?

MOTHER

A glass of water, sweetheart.

BUDDY

No, I meant—

(*But maybe the water would be quicker. He rushes to the bar and pours a glass of water*)

MOTHER

I've got no luck. I never had any and I never will.

BUDDY

(Rushes back with glass)

Here, Mom.

MOTHER

(Takes a sip)

That just makes me nauseous.

(He takes glass and puts it on fireplace bench left)

Let me catch my breath.

BUDDY

Maybe you need some fresh air, Mom. Outside?

MOTHER

(Rises)

Just let me sit a few minutes . . . Where's Alan?

BUDDY

Out. On business. Do you feel any better?

MOTHER

When did I ever feel better?

BUDDY

Mom, I hope you understand, but I've got this appointment tonight.

MOTHER

Did you have dinner yet?

BUDDY

What? Dinner? Yes. Yes, I had a sandwich.

MOTHER

A sandwich? For supper? That's how you start the minute you're away?

BUDDY

I'm not hungry, Mom. You see, I've got this appointment . . .

MOTHER

What'd you have, one of those greasy hamburgers?

BUDDY

No. Roast beef. I had a big roast beef sandwich.

MOTHER

That's not enough for you. Let me make you some eggs.

BUDDY

I don't want any eggs.

MOTHER

Look at this place. Look at the dirt.

BUDDY

It's all right, Mom.

MOTHER

Sure. Boys. I'll bet no one's been in here to clean in a year.

BUDDY

(*He might as well tell her*)

Mom, will you listen to me. I'm . . . I'm . . . I'm expecting a girl here in a few minutes.

MOTHER

To clean?

BUDDY

(*Exasperated*)

No, not to clean . . . She's a friend of mine.

MOTHER

From our neighborhood?

BUDDY

No, you don't know her. She's . . . er . . . a girl I knew in school. We're writing a story together.

MOTHER

Then let me make you some appetizers.

BUDDY

We don't want any appetizers.

MOTHER

Buddy, I've got to talk to you about your father.

BUDDY

Can't we do it tomorrow? She's going to be here any second.

MOTHER

What's the matter? She's more important than me?

BUDDY

Mom, no one's more important than you.

MOTHER

How can you say that when you worry me like this? I know you. You won't eat unless the food's in front of you.

BUDDY

No one eats unless the food's in front of them. Mom, I haven't got time . . .

MOTHER

 (*Hurt*)

You want me to go, I'll go.

BUDDY

Mom, please don't be hurt. I didn't want to have this meeting. It came up unexpectedly. But I have to go through with it.

MOTHER

Buddy, your father's going to be home in a few minutes. You should have heard him on the phone before about Alan. If the operator was listening, there'll be a man there in the morning to rip it off the wall.

BUDDY

I can't discuss this with you now.

MOTHER

No, but for girls you've got time.

 (*Sits right center chair*)

BUDDY

It's not a girl. It's . . . a . . . meeting. About a story we're writing. It may go on till two o'clock in the morning.

MOTHER

Without appetizers?

BUDDY

We don't need appetizers!

MOTHER

 (*Crosses to him*)

Wait'll he reads that letter. Wait'll he finds out you're gone. Remember what he did when Alan left?

BUDDY

I know, Mom. He was very upset.

MOTHER

Upset? I'll never forget it. He came home from work at three
o'clock, went into his room, put on his pajamas and got into
bed to die . . . Four days he stayed in bed. He just laid there
waiting to die.

BUDDY

But he didn't die, Mom. He put on weight.

MOTHER

Don't think he wasn't disappointed . . . He was plenty hurt
by Alan leaving, believe me. He thought by now Alan would
be married, have a grandchild. Who knows if he'll ever get
married. And now you.

BUDDY

Mom, please—

MOTHER

I know what he's going to say tonight. He'll blame it all on
me. He'll say I was too easy with the both of you. He'll say,
"Because of you my sister Gussie has two grandchildren and
all I've got is a bum and a letter" . . . I know him.

BUDDY

Look, Mom. How about if I come home tomorrow night for
dinner? And I'll have a long talk with Dad about everything.
Okay?

MOTHER

Tomorrow? By tomorrow he'll be in bed again writing out his
will. He'll be on the phone saying good-by to his family.

BUDDY

He won't, Mom. He just gets very dramatic sometimes.

MOTHER

Maybe I am too easygoing. Maybe if I were like some mothers
who forbid their children to do everything, I'd be better off
today.

BUDDY

No, Mom. You're the best mother I ever had . . . Do you feel
any better?

MOTHER

How do I know? I feel too sick to tell.

BUDDY

Really, a good night's sleep and you'll feel wonderful. Take something before you go to bed. Some warm milk.

MOTHER

Who buys milk now that you're not there.

BUDDY

Then buy some.

MOTHER

Maybe I'll be better off if I take a hot bath.

BUDDY

That's the girl.

MOTHER

I'll probably pass out right in the tub.

BUDDY

No you won't. Why do you get so emotional all the time?

MOTHER

I don't look for it, believe me, darling.

BUDDY

Mom, everything's going to be all right.
   (*He half lifts her to her feet*)
Sleep tight.
   (*He kisses her forehead*)

MOTHER

I feel better knowing at least you'll be there tomorrow.

BUDDY

For dinner. I promise.
   (*He starts upstage*)

MOTHER

   (*She stops*)
. . . What'll I make?

BUDDY

   (*Coming down to her*)
What?

MOTHER

For dinner? What do you want to eat?

BUDDY

Anything. I don't care. Good night, Mom.

MOTHER

I want to make something you like now that you're not home.

BUDDY

I like everything. Roast beef, okay?

MOTHER

All right, good.

(*He starts upstage. She starts, then stops*)

You had roast beef tonight.

(*He comes back*)

BUDDY

(*Beside himself with anxiety*)

I can eat it again.

MOTHER

I could get a turkey. A big turkey.

BUDDY

Okay! Turkey! Wonderful!

MOTHER

It doesn't really pay for one night.

BUDDY

(*He can't take it any more. He practically screams*)

Mom, for Pete's sakes, it doesn't matter.

MOTHER

(*Near tears*)

What are you yelling? I'm only trying to make you happy. Who do I cook for, myself? I haven't eaten anything besides coffee for ten years.

BUDDY

I'm sorry, Mom.

MOTHER

Oh, I've got that stick in the heart again.

(*Sits right center chair*)

BUDDY

You're just upset.

MOTHER

No. I ate lamb chops tonight. They never agree with me.

BUDDY

Oh, boy.

MOTHER

Darling, do you have an Alka-Seltzer?

BUDDY

Alka-Seltzer? I don't know . . . Wait a minute. I'll look in the kitchen.

  (*He rushes off madly to the kitchen right*)

MOTHER

  (*She rubs her stomach*)

She wished it on me. His sister Gussie wished it on me.

  (BUDDY *comes running back out*)

BUDDY

There isn't any here.

MOTHER

Sure. Boys. You wouldn't have water if you didn't have a faucet.

BUDDY

Mom, make anything you want. Turkey. Roast beef. I'll be home tomorrow night. Now why don't you go home and relax. Take a cab.

MOTHER

It's starting to rain. Where am I going to get a cab?

BUDDY

I'll get you one, okay?

MOTHER

All right. Let me sit a few minutes.

BUDDY

A few minutes?

  (*He can't wait any longer*)

Mom, I'll get the doorman to get you a cab.

  (*Runs up to door*)

Do you want to wait in the lobby?

MOTHER

You don't have to run out.

BUDDY

I'll be right back. In two minutes.

(*And he is gone in a flash*)

MOTHER

Don't get overheated . . . Who am I talking to?

(*She looks around the apartment and shakes her head disapprovingly. Puts bag on chair, unbuttons coat . . . She gets up, crosses to the coffee table, empties one ash tray into the other. Then starts to cross with the refuse into the kitchen when the phone rings. She turns and goes to the phone*) (*Into phone*)

Hello? . . . Who? . . . No, he isn't. To whom am I speaking to, please? Meltzer? Martin Meltzer . . . No, this is Alan's mother . . . What? . . . Why should I kid about a thing like that? . . . No, I'm positive he's not here . . . A message? . . . Wait. I'll get a pencil.

(*She looks for a pencil. There is none on the table, so she runs quickly to the left cabinet, then upstage cabinet, sofa, table and looks frantically for a pencil. There is none to be found. She runs back quickly to the phone*)

Go on, I'll remember. Talk fast so I could write it down as soon as you're finished . . . "Extremely important. Your wife just came in unexpectedly from Atlantic City and is on her way to the Hotel Croyden so Alan should be sure *not* to come with those certain parties." Yes, I have it . . . I do . . . I can't repeat it to you, I'm trying to remember it . . . Mr. Meltzer, Hotel Croyden . . . Yes . . . Don't talk any more, I'm going to write it down quick. Good-by.

(*She hangs up*)

Some message. That's a book, not a message.

(*She starts to look for a pencil again*)

Where's a pencil? They don't have Alka-Seltzer, they're gonna have a pencil?

(*She crosses right toward counter*)

(The phone rings)
Suddenly I'm an answering service.
(She answers phone)
Hello? . . . No, he isn't . . . This is Alan's mother . . . Why
should I kid about a thing like that? . . . To whom am I
speaking to please? . . . Who? . . . Chickie? . . . That's a
name? . . . Chickie Parker . . . You forgot whose hotel?
. . . Mr. Meltzer's? Where do I know that name from? . . .
Oh, for God sakes, he just called. With a message to Alan.
Something about Atlantic City. I think he said Alan shouldn't
go there . . . I don't know what it means either. I'm not a sec-
retary. I'm a mother . . . without a pencil . . . The hotel?
. . . Yes, he did mention it . . . I think it was the Parker . . .
Oh, that's *your* name . . . Wait. Oh, yes. The Croyden . . .
A message for Alan? I can only try, darling . . . "Chickie was
detained but she's on her way to the Croyden now." Yes.
You're welcome. Good-by.
*(She hangs up. She crosses upstage to desk area, looking
for a pencil)*
There must be some carrying on here. Their father should
only know . . . A businessman and a college boy and they
don't have a pencil.
(She starts right and the phone rings again)
Oh, for God's sakes.
(The phone rings again)
All right, all right, what do you want from me?
(She rushes quickly to the phone and picks it up)
Yes? . . . Who? . . . Who did you want, please? . . . No,
he's out. This is Alan's mother . . . Listen, don't start that
with me . . . Who is this? . . . Connie what? . . . Again
with a message . . . Miss, can't you write it down, I don't
have a pencil . . . You what? . . . Yes . . . Yes . . . Yes . . .
You're welcome . . . Good-by.
(She hangs up)
Good-by, go home, good luck, who knows what she said.
(Sits sofa and cries)

Who tells him to have so many phone calls? . . . It's disgusting.

(*The phone rings. She screams*)

What do you want from my life?

(*She just stares at the phone. It continues to ring*)

I wouldn't pick it up now if it stood on its head.

(*It continues to ring*)

Oh, I'm so nauseous.

(*She can't stand it any longer. She picks it up, but she yells at it angrily*)

Hello? . . . What do you want? . . . Who is this? . . . Alan who? . . . Oh, Alan . . .

(*She starts to cry*)

It's Mother.

(*She sits*)

What am I doing here? . . . I'm answering your phone calls . . . He's outside getting me a subway . . . I mean a taxi . . . No, there's no one else here . . . Who called? . . . The whole world called . . . First a man called . . . Meltzer? . . . No, it didn't sound like that . . .

(*The door opens and* BUDDY *rushes in*)

BUDDY

Okay, Mom.

MOTHER

(*Into phone*)

Oh, I've got to go now. Buddy is here with the cab. Talk to Buddy.

BUDDY

I've got the cab. It's waiting outside.

MOTHER

Here.

(*Hands him phone*)

BUDDY

Who is that?

MOTHER

Alan.

(*She gets up and hands phone to* BUDDY *and crosses right to get bag*)
Here!

BUDDY

(*Taking phone*)
Hello, Alan? . . . What's wrong? I don't know who called, I was outside.
(*To* MOTHER)
Mom, did someone call?

MOTHER

I gave all the messages to Alan. I don't want to keep the taxi waiting. Good-by, sweetheart.
(*She starts to door*)

BUDDY

Mom, who called? A girl?

MOTHER

Yes, darling. Good-by.

BUDDY

What did she say?

MOTHER

I don't remember.
(*She opens door*)

BUDDY

Why didn't you write it down?

MOTHER

Don't *you* start with me . . . This must be costing a fortune. I only hope I don't pass out in the taxi!
(*She goes*)

BUDDY

Mom, wait . . .
(*Into phone*)
Hello, Alan . . . I don't know. I can't make head or tail out of her . . . Where are you? . . . No, she didn't get here yet . . . Lousy, that's how I feel . . . I already had a drink. It doesn't help . . . Hey, wait a minute. Who am I again? . . . Oscar *Wol*heim? . . . *Manheim!* Oscar Manheim . . . Oh,

boy . . . Look, Alan. I changed my mind. I can't go through
with it. I'm going out. Yes. Now. Well . . . I'll leave her a
note from you . . . I'm sorry. Good-by.

(*He hangs up*)

That's it. I'll leave her a note. That's all.

(*He quickly starts to search for a pencil and paper. He
looks in the shelves under downstage left cabinet and takes
out container with two dozen pencils*)

Eight thousand pencils and no paper.

(*He crosses to table behind sofa and finds piece of paper.
He sits sofa and starts to write and repeats aloud*)

"Dear Peggy . . . More bad news . . . Paul . . .

(*Momentarily forgets name*)

Manheim . . . is . . . dead! . . . Love . . . Alan"

(*He puts down pencil, then crosses to door. Reads letter
again as he bends down to leave it under door. The front
bell rings. He gasps. The bell rings again. He throws up
his hands in despair and then opens door. PEGGY stands
there ravishingly dressed. She looks utterly fantastic*)

PEGGY

Hi. I'm Peggy Evans.

(*She walks in. He closes door*)

I'm not disturbing you or anything, am I?

BUDDY

(*He looks at her, overwhelmed by her pulchritude, follows
her downstage*)

No . . . not at all.

(*He is in a state of semi-shock*)

PEGGY

(*Sitting on sofa*)

Alan said you wanted to meet me. I hope you forgive the way
I look. I've been in a car all day . . . I must be a mess.

BUDDY

No . . . You look . . . very neat.

(*He tears up the note and puts pieces in his pocket*)

PEGGY

Thanks . . . Coming from you, that's something.
   (*She crosses to him*)
It's a shame you couldn't get up to the ski lodge.

BUDDY

What ski lodge?

PEGGY

In New Hampshire. Or Vermont. I'm not very good at names.
In fact, I'm afraid I've forgotten yours.

BUDDY

Oh . . . It's . . . *Man*heim.

PEGGY

That's right. Mr. Manheim.

BUDDY

Jack Man—heim . . . No, not Jack.

PEGGY

That's right, Jack.

BUDDY

Yes, Jack . . . won't you sit down?
   (*Indicating right center chair*)

PEGGY

Thank you . . .
   (*She sits on sofa*)
I understand you had some problem at the studio.

BUDDY

Oh, yes . . . we did.

PEGGY

What was it?
   (*She takes a cigarette and lights it*)

BUDDY

It was . . . er . . .
   (*He sees flame*)
Er . . . we had a . . . fire.

PEGGY

Who?

BUDDY

I beg your pardon?

PEGGY

Who did you have to fire?

BUDDY

No, no. *A* fire. Part of the studio burned down.

PEGGY

Oh? Was anyone hurt?

BUDDY

No . . . just a few extras . . . Say, would you like a drink?

PEGGY

Oooh, like a transfusion. I don't mind admitting it, but I'm nervous.

BUDDY

You're nervous? What would you like?

PEGGY

What are you having?

BUDDY

(This one is easy. He tosses it off grandly)

Oh . . . scotch and ginger ale.

PEGGY

Oh, that's cute. I mean what are you *really* having?

BUDDY

(Embarrassed)

I don't know. What are you having?

PEGGY

Grand Marnier.

BUDDY

Grandma who?

PEGGY

Grand Marnier. It's French. You know, a liquoor.

BUDDY

Oh . . .

(He crosses up to bar and looks for it. He picks up a scotch bottle)

No, I don't see any.

PEGGY

Oh, scotch'll be fine.

(*He pours drinks*)

I suppose you've heard it before, but you look awfully young for a producer.

BUDDY

(*Crossing left of her*)

Oh, do I?

PEGGY

To look at you I'd say you were only about twenty-six, but I bet I'm way off.

BUDDY

Oh, way off.

(*Hands her drink and sits left of her*)

Well, here we are.

PEGGY

What should we drink to?

BUDDY

Anything you like.

PEGGY

Let's make a silent toast.

BUDDY

Okay.

(*They both close their eyes, take a beat, she opens hers, nudges him, he opens his eyes, clink glasses and drink*)

PEGGY

(*Makes herself comfortable, puts down glass and snuffs out cigarette*)

Well, now . . . down to business.

BUDDY

Huh?

PEGGY

I suppose you want to know what I've done.

BUDDY

Not necessarily.

PEGGY

I'll be perfectly frank with you. I've never been in a picture before.

BUDDY

Is that so?

PEGGY

But I'm not totally inexperienced.

BUDDY

So Alan told me.

PEGGY

Last summer when I was on the Coast I did an "Untouchables."

BUDDY

No kidding?

PEGGY

I was a dead body. They fished me out of the river.

BUDDY

I think I saw that.

PEGGY

Lots of people did. I got loads of work from it. But it's not what I really want to do. That's why I'm taking acting class. With Felix Ungar. He lives in this building. Right under this apartment. In fact *that's* how I met Alan.

(*She puts her hand on his right knee*)

I rang the wrong bell one night.

(BUDDY *looks down at his knee and laughs almost hysterically*)

BUDDY

How about that?

PEGGY

And look how it turned out. Through a silly mistake, I'm being auditioned by one of the biggest producers (*taking hand off knee*) in the business. Life is funny, isn't it?

BUDDY

(*Puts drink down and rises crossing right*)

Hysterical.

PEGGY

(Rises—crosses below coffee table)

Well, is there anything you'd like me to do?

BUDDY

What?

PEGGY

Do. Read a scene? Or kind of take on a character like in class. Or is just talking like this enough?

BUDDY

Oh, it's plenty. To tell the truth, I'm a little tired.

(Sits right center chair)

PEGGY

Oh, from the trip. Would you like me to massage your think muscle?

BUDDY

Huh?

PEGGY

Here!

(She indicates her temple. She goes to where he's sitting, and stands over him)

Just close your eyes and put your head back.

BUDDY

I don't think . . .

PEGGY

I'm very good at this. Now just relax . . .

(He does)

. . . and try and forget about the picture business.

(She massages)

No, I can feel it. You're still thinking about the studio.

BUDDY

No, I'm not. I swear I'm not.

(The phone rings. He jumps up)

PEGGY

Are you expecting anyone?

BUDDY

Me? No! No!

(*It rings again, angrily*)

No, I'll get it. I'll get it.

(*He crosses to phone quickly and picks it up. Into phone*)

Hello! . . . *Dad!!!* . . . I'm sorry. I didn't mean to yell . . .
What? . . . now? . . . Look, Dad, I'll come downstairs,
okay? . . . Dad? . . . Dad? . . . Oh, boy!

(*He hangs up*)

PEGGY

Is anything wrong?

BUDDY

What? Oh, yeah . . . It's . . . it's someone I don't want to see
. . . A writer . . .

PEGGY

Dad? It sounded like it was your father.

BUDDY

Oh! Oh, no. That's just a nickname. Dad. You know, like
Ernest Hemingway is Poppa.

PEGGY

Oh! Is Dad coming up?

BUDDY

Yeah, Dad's coming up . . . Look, would you do me a big, big
favor? I've got to be alone with him for a few minutes . . . To
talk about script changes.

PEGGY

I understand. I could go up and get that bottle of Grand
Marnier.

BUDDY

(*That's inspirational*)

That's it. Would you do that?

PEGGY

Of course.

(*She starts for the door*)

BUDDY

(He stops her)
Not that way!

PEGGY

What?

BUDDY

I don't want him to know I'm auditioning someone else. He's already got someone in mind.

PEGGY

Oh, I appreciate that. Thanks an awful lot, Mr. Manheim. *(She kisses him and exits through the kitchen door. He starts right to make sure she has gone. He looks at his jacket, unbuttons it, takes it off, throws it into bedroom and closes door. He runs downstage grabs the two glasses from coffee table and puts them on bar. He starts right, stops, looks at glasses. Picks one up and examines it for lipstick, takes out his handkerchief, wipes lipstick off, puts glass on bar. As he wipes his own mouth with handkerchief, doorbell rings. He frantically tries to jam handkerchief into pocket and can't. Doorbell rings again. Panicky, he throws handkerchief out window left. He grabs a large book from upstage bookshelf, opens it, goes to door, book in hand, composes himself as if he had been reading all evening and opens door. There stands his FATHER, with the letter in his hand)*

BUDDY

Hello, Dad.
(The FATHER walks in, holds up the letter to BUDDY's face, to indicate he got it, then he walks into the apartment. BUDDY follows left of him)
Are you all right, Dad? . . . Is anything wrong?
(The FATHER stares ahead speechless. He has taken letter out of envelope and now holds it in front of BUDDY's face)
I—I didn't think you'd be coming down tonight . . . I was going to have a long talk with you in the morning . . . at the plant . . . and then I told Mother I'd be home for dinner tomorrow night . . . so you and I could sit down and talk some

more . . . and I could explain how I . . . Dad, you're angry, aren't you . . .

FATHER

Me? Angry. Why should I be angry?

BUDDY

About the letter.

FATHER

(*Looks at him*)
What letter?

BUDDY

This letter. The letter I wrote you.

FATHER

No, no. You didn't write this letter. Someone I don't know wrote this letter. Not you. You, I know. This person I never met.

BUDDY

Dad, don't you think it would be better if we waited until to-morrow, when we're both—calmer? Dad, I meant to have a long talk with you about this.

FATHER

Talk? What's there to talk about?
(*He still holds up letter*)
It's signed, sealed and delivered. The Declaration of Inde-pendence . . . What's there to talk about?

BUDDY

Dad, I think you're too upset now to discuss this logically.

FATHER

Oh, I expected it.
(*Puts letter in envelope*)
You hang around your brother long enough it was bound to happen. So what's the windup. My sister Gussie has two grandchildren and I have a bum and a letter.

BUDDY

Dad, this didn't suddenly happen. I tried to explain how I felt the other night. But you wouldn't listen.

FATHER

(*He starts to sit and jumps up*)

Don't try and tell me I wouldn't listen. That's all I did was
listen.

(*Crosses left*)

BUDDY

But every time I would start to say something, you would walk
out of the room.

FATHER

If you showed me a little respect, then maybe I would listen.

BUDDY

Dad, you're not making any sense.

FATHER

I'm not making sense? Very nice. Very nice talk to a father.

BUDDY

What do you want me to say?

FATHER

I want to hear from your own lips . . . nicely . . . why such a
young boy can't live at home with his parents.

BUDDY

Young boy?

FATHER

(*Holding up a warning finger*)

Nicely!

BUDDY

Dad, I'm twenty-one.

FATHER

(*Noncommittal*)

You're twenty-one.

BUDDY

You say it as if you don't believe me. I was twenty-one yesterday, wasn't I?

FATHER

(*Shrugs*)

Whatever you say.

BUDDY

What do you mean whatever I say?

FATHER

(Finger up again)

Nicely!

BUDDY

All right. *I say* I was twenty-one. That's old enough to make your own decisions in life. When *you* were twenty-one, you were already married, weren't you?

FATHER

You were there?

BUDDY

No, I wasn't there. You told me yourself.

FATHER

Those days were altogether different.

(Crosses away left)

I was working when I was eleven years old.

(Turns to him)

I didn't go to camp.

BUDDY

What's camp got to do with all this???

FATHER

(Threatening)

I'll walk right out of here!

BUDDY

Dad, all right. I don't mean to be disrespectful, but your answers never match my questions.

FATHER

(Crossing above and right of Buddy)

Oh, that too? I don't talk fancy enough for you like your brother and his show business friends.

BUDDY

That's what I mean. Who said anything about show business?

FATHER

Well, that's where he is all day, isn't he? Backstage at some burlesque house.

BUDDY

They haven't had burlesque in New York in twenty years.

FATHER

He hasn't put in a day's work in twenty years. And now I suppose I can expect that of you.

BUDDY

No, Dad. I'll work there as long as you want me to . . . No matter how I feel about it.

FATHER

What do you mean, no matter how you feel?

BUDDY

Well, Dad, I never had a chance to try anything else. I had two years of college, then the Army, and then right into the business. Maybe it's not the right field for me.

FATHER

Not the right field?

(*He addresses an imaginary listener in right center chair*)
I give the boy the biggest artificial fruit manufacturing house in the East, he tells me *not the right field*. Ha!

(*He sits right center chair*)

BUDDY

I don't know if I've got any talent . . . but . . . I've always toyed with the idea of becoming a writer.

FATHER

A writer? What kind of writer? Letters?

(*He holds up letter*)

Letters you write beautiful. I don't know who's going to buy them, but they're terrific.

BUDDY

But supposing I'm good? I'm not even getting a chance to find out. Supposing I could write plays . . . for television or the theater?

FATHER

Plays can close.

(*Crossing to him*)

Television you turn off. Wax fruit lays in the bowl till you're a hundred.

BUDDY

But business doesn't stimulate me, Dad. I don't have fun.

FATHER

You don't have fun? I'll put in music, you can dance while you work.

BUDDY

Dad, forget about the business for now. I'll stay. All I want now is your permission for me to live here on my own.

FATHER

(Puts letter in coat pocket)

All right, let me ask you a question. If you were in my place, if you were my father, with conditions in the world as they are today, with juvenile delinquency, with the stories you read in the papers about the crazy parties that go on, the drinking and whatnot . . . would you let *your* son leave home?

BUDDY

Yes!

FATHER

That's no answer!

BUDDY

Dad, it just doesn't seem as if we're ever going to understand each other.

FATHER

How can we? You listen to your brother more than you listen to me.

BUDDY

That's not true.

FATHER

Do you deny that he's the one who put this bug in your mouth about leaving home?

BUDDY

In your ear, Dad.

FATHER

What?

BUDDY

Bug in your ear.

FATHER

Excuse my ignorance, Mr. Writer.

BUDDY

I wasn't making fun of you.

FATHER

Why not? Your brother does.

BUDDY

No, he doesn't.

FATHER

He doesn't, heh? I can imagine the things he must tell you. You'll learn plenty from him, believe me, plenty. At least you I had hopes for. Alan I could never talk to. But you, you were always good. I could take you anywhere. I could take you visiting, you would sit on a chair for three hours, you wouldn't hear a peep out of you. I remember I used to say, give Aunt Gussie a kiss. You'd go right over and give Aunt Gussie a kiss. But the older one. I chased him all over Brooklyn one day because he wouldn't give Aunt Gussie a kiss . . . What was so terrible to give Aunt Gussie a kiss?

BUDDY

I guess it was that hat she wore. You always had to kiss her through a veil.

FATHER

You see how you take his side.

BUDDY

I wasn't taking his side.

FATHER

No, heh? What's the use talking to you. You'll do what he says in the end anyway. If you want to become a bum like him, that's your affair.

BUDDY

Why is Alan a bum?

FATHER

Is he married?

BUDDY

No.

FATHER

Then he's a bum!

BUDDY

Dad, you really never had any problems with me before, have
you? Won't you trust me now?

FATHER

  (*He sighs*)
All right, you want trust. I'll give you trust.

BUDDY

What do you mean?

FATHER

There's a disagreement here. A dispute. We'll arbitrate.

BUDDY

That's all I've been asking of you.

FATHER

I've heard your side. You've heard my side. If you want, we'll
give it a six-month trial period. Fairer than that, I can't be.

BUDDY

I think that's very fair, Dad. Six months is fine.
  (*Crossing left*)

FATHER

Then it's settled. You'll come home and live for six months . . .

BUDDY

Come home?
  (*Shouts, crossing to him*)
You don't want to give me a trial. You don't want to be fair
. . . You just—just—

FATHER

  (*Rises and shakes upstage hand*)
Don't you raise your voice. You're not too big to get a good slap
across the face.

BUDDY

I'm sorry, Dad.

FATHER

I never thought I'd live to see this day. That a son would talk to his father like this. I've been some terrible father to you, haven't I?

BUDDY

No, Dad. You've been a wonderful father. Just meet me half-way. Please . . . What do you say?

FATHER

(Crosses left of him)

I'll . . . I'll let you know.

BUDDY

What do you mean, you'll let me know?

FATHER

I'm not rushing into any decisions hell mell . . . I'll go home and think about it. If you want, you can stay here tonight, I won't argue. But tomorrow, you'll come home for dinner and we'll see what we'll see.

BUDDY

All right, that'll be fine. Good night, Dad.

(He starts upstage)

FATHER

You need any money?

BUDDY

No, I've got plenty.

(Comes back)

FATHER

Where are you going to sleep?

BUDDY

On the sofa.

FATHER

That's some place to sleep.

BUDDY

Dad, I'll be all right. I'll see you tomorrow. I promise.

FATHER

You don't have to promise. You say you'll be there, I trust you.

BUDDY

Thanks, Dad. Good night.

(*Starts up again*)

FATHER

(*Just about to leave, when he stops and turns*)

Oh, wait a minute.

BUDDY

What's the matter?

FATHER

I want to call your mother. Tell her everything's all right. I
know she's worried.

(*He crosses to phone*)

BUDDY

(*Crossing and sits down center chair*)

Oh, boy!

(*The* FATHER *dials, sighing, in* BUDDY's *direction*)

FATHER

(*Into phone*)

Hello? . . . Jezebel? . . . Is Mrs. Baker home? . . . Oh! I
wonder where she is? . . . Listen, Jezebel, before you go
home, I want you to write down a message for her . . . All
right, get a pencil . . .

(*Suddenly* PEGGY *comes out from the kitchen. She wears a
topcoat.* BUDDY *rises as she enters*)

PEGGY

Excuse me, but I'm all out of Grand Marnier too, I'll run down
to the liquor store and get some.

(*To* FATHER)

Hello, Dad!

(*She goes back out kitchen door*)

(*The* FATHER *stares after her dumfounded.* BUDDY *is in a
state of shock. The* FATHER *turns slowly back to the phone*)

FATHER

Hello, Jezebel? . . . Tell Mrs. Baker I'm with the bum! . . .
The twenty-one-year-old bum!

(He slams the phone down, turns and points an accusing finger at BUDDY*)*

Bum!

BUDDY

Dad . . .

FATHER

Bum!

BUDDY

Let me explain . . .

FATHER

Bum!

BUDDY

Please . . .

FATHER

Twenty-one years old! You're a bigger bum than your brother is right now and you've still got twelve years to go!

BUDDY

Dad, please.

(The front door suddenly opens. ALAN *walks in and sees the* FATHER.*)*

ALAN

Dad!!

FATHER

Ah, the other bum. Come on in. We're having a party.

ALAN

What are you doing here?

FATHER

I was invited to dinner. That's some cook you have in there.

ALAN

Where?

BUDDY

(Defeated)

In the kitchen.

ALAN

What? . . .

(To BUDDY*)*

Well, didn't you explain? That she was waiting for me?

FATHER

I don't need you to make up stories.
   (*Crosses to* BUDDY)
I've got Tennessee Williams for that.
   (*The phone rings.* FATHER *starts out*)

ALAN

Dad, wait. I want to talk to you.
   (*He crosses quickly to the phone*)

FATHER

I've heard enough.
   (*He starts to go*)

ALAN

   (*Into phone*)
Hello? . . . Oh, Mr. Meltzer.

FATHER

   (*Stops*)
Meltzer? What does he want?

ALAN

   (*Into phone*)
Now, please. Calm down. I tried to explain. There was a mix-up somewhere.

FATHER

What's wrong?

ALAN

Nothing, Dad. Nothing.
   (*Into phone*)
What? . . . Well, how should I know your wife was coming in? . . . I didn't get any message from my mother.

FATHER

   (*Crosses to him*)
What are you talking about?

ALAN

   (*Into phone*)
If I can just talk to your wife . . . Mr. Meltzer, there's no need for a lawsuit.

FATHER

Lawsuit? What lawsuit?

ALAN

Dad, wait a minute . . .
  (*Into phone*)
Mr. Meltzer . . .

FATHER

Give me that phone.
  (*Grabs phone and brightly says*)
Hello? Meltzer? This is Mr. Baker, senior. What's the trouble?

ALAN

He's hysterical, Dad. Don't listen to him.

FATHER

Your wife and *who* rang the doorbell together? What French
girl? . . . But who arranged such a thing? . . . I see . . .
  (*Turns to* ALAN)
I see . . . Good-by.
  (*He hands phone to* ALAN, *who hangs up, and starts for
  door.* ALAN *follows*)

ALAN

Dad, if you'd just listen for five minutes . . . Dad!!!!! Dad,
Dad . . . please say something!
  (*The* FATHER *crosses past them in silence. He turns on
  raised foyer and speaks calmly*)

FATHER

May you and your brother live and be well. God bless you, all
the luck in the world, you should know nothing but happiness. If I ever speak to either one of you again, my tongue
should fall out!
  (*He opens the door and goes*)

  (*The two brothers stand there looking at each other help-
  lessly*)

BUDDY

  (*Crosses right to fireplace*)
I knew it. I knew this would happen.

ALAN

  (*Concerned*)
Do you think he means it?

(ALAN *takes off coat and puts it on left handrail*)

BUDDY

Means it? In ten minutes he'll be home, giving the rest of my clothes to the janitor.

ALAN

(*Crosses downstage right of sofa*)

I never saw him this mad.

(*Crossing down*)

Not since the day he chased me all over Brooklyn when I wouldn't give Aunt Gussie a kiss.

BUDDY

Oh, he's mad all right. And he means it.

(*Crosses left to him*)

We're *fired*.

ALAN

(*Musing*)

But how can he get along without us?

BUDDY

And he was almost out the door. And then that fruitcake walks in and says, "Hello, Dad" . . . His mustache almost fell off.

ALAN

(*Sits sofa*)

I'm sorry, kid. I didn't mean to get you involved.

BUDDY

It's not your fault.

ALAN

I thought I was doing you a favor . . . Well, it's over with anyway.

BUDDY

What's over? She's coming back with a French bottle to do silly little things.

ALAN

She is?

BUDDY

She gets me all crazy. Suppose I do something nutty, like signing her to a five-year contract? . . .

(*Doorbell rings*)

I can't face her again, Alan. Please.

ALAN

All right, never mind. I'll take over. Go on out to a movie.

BUDDY

(*Grabs his coat from under sofa*)

That's a great idea. Maybe one of my pictures is playing around.

(*Doorbell rings again. He exits through kitchen right. ALAN opens door; CONNIE stands there with valise*)

ALAN

Connie!

(*Closes door. She puts down case and gives Alan long kiss interrupting his "Wha . . ." then when she releases him*)

CONNIE

Me no Connie. Me Jane. You Tarzan. Jane come to swing with Tarzan in tree.

ALAN

What's in that suitcase?

CONNIE

The rest of my merchandise.

(*She takes off her coat. Puts it on right handrail*)

ALAN

You're drunk.

(*Crossing away right*)

CONNIE

On one martini?

ALAN

You get loaded just ordering one.

CONNIE

Now, then, the bedroom. It's in that direction, isn't it?

(*She picks up suitcase and starts for bedroom*)

ALAN

You stay out of there. What's come over you?

CONNIE

Nothing, darling. I gave you a choice and you made it.

ALAN
Connie, you can't go to Europe. I won't let you.

(*Act III*)

ALAN

What?

CONNIE

Wonderful service, isn't it? You don't even have to pick it up.
We deliver.

ALAN

You're not drunk. You're crazy.

CONNIE

(*Puts down suitcase and crosses right stalking him as he
backs away*)

Just think of it, darling? We're going to live together, love
together. Fun, fun, fun. Sin, sin, sin.

ALAN

Connie, you're scaring the hell out of me.

CONNIE

You don't even have to say you love me. And when you get
bored, just kick me out and give me a letter of recommenda-
tion.

ALAN

Will you cut it out? It's not funny any more.
(*Breaks away left*)

CONNIE

I don't understand, Alan. Isn't this what you want? Isn't this
what you asked for?

ALAN

No.

CONNIE

No?

ALAN

That's right, no. I said I could see nothing wrong for two
young people who were very fond of each other to have a
healthy, normal relationship. But I see no reason to turn this
affair into a . . . foreign art movie.

CONNIE

Good heavens, sir. I must be in the wrong apartment.

ALAN

Look, I told you before. I'm not denying anything. Six nights a week I'm Leonard Lover. But with you . . . well, you're different.

CONNIE

Careful, Alan. You're on the brink of committing yourself.

ALAN

Who's keeping it a secret? I love you.

CONNIE

You weren't very sure.

ALAN

I am now. If I can turn down an offer like this with a girl like you, I must be in love.

CONNIE

Well, then . . . where does that leave us?

ALAN

. . . I don't know.

CONNIE

(Sits right arm of right center chair)
You don't know?

ALAN

(Crossing to her)
Look honey, you've got to give me a chance to think. A lot of things have happened tonight. I just lost my job.

CONNIE

I thought you worked for your father.

ALAN

We must be in a hell of a recession. He just let two sons go . . . Oh, Connie, don't you see . . .

CONNIE

No, I don't see. You love me but you won't marry me, and you love me too much to live with me.

ALAN

(Crosses around chair to right of it)
I know. I can't figure it out either.

CONNIE

(*Angry*)

I see. Well, I'm sorry, Alan, but I can't spend the rest of my life waiting in the hallway.

(*She gets up and crosses to center*)

ALAN

Wait a minute.

CONNIE

For what? I either come in or go out. You want me or you don't. Yes or no.

ALAN

Why can't things be like they were before?

CONNIE

It's too late. We've raised the stakes.

ALAN

Who made you the dealer all of a sudden?

CONNIE

If the game is too big, Alan, get out.

ALAN

I see. A brilliant maneuver, General. You've got me cornered. Very well, I surrender.

CONNIE

I don't take prisoners.

(*She goes to foyer*)

ALAN

(*Angry*)

I mean it. If that's what you want, I'll marry you.

CONNIE

(*Grabs coat. Puts over left arm*)

If that's the way you'll marry me, I don't want it.

ALAN

(*Crossing to her*)

Connie, wait. Where are you going?

CONNIE

(*Putting on coat*)

Right now I want to be about a thirty-five-*dollar* taxi ride away from you.

ALAN

(*Sincerely. Crossing to her*)

Connie, wait . . . I don't want you to leave.

CONNIE

(*She's made up her mind*)

I'm sorry.

ALAN

You mean I won't see you again?

CONNIE

I don't know. Maybe if you get lonely enough.

(*The phone rings*)

You probably won't have much chance tonight. Start in the morning.

(*Phone rings again. Picks up suitcase*)

ALAN

Connie, wait.

CONNIE

Answer your phone, Alan. It's the second platoon.

(*Phone rings again*)

ALAN

(*He picks up phone*)

Hello . . . Oh, Mom.

(*To* CONNIE)

Connie, it's my mother.

CONNIE

Your mother? Oh, come on, Alan.

(*She opens door*)

ALAN

Why should I kid about a thing like that?

CONNIE

Good-by.

(*And she's gone closing door behind her*)

ALAN

Connie . . . Connie, wait.

(*Back into phone. He sits*)

Hello, Mom? . . . What's wrong? Did Dad get home

yet? . . . Aunt Gussie's? . . . Well, don't worry about it. He'll probably just sleep there tonight. He'll be home tomorrow when he calms down . . . Mom, please don't cry . . . All right, look, I'll come up and sleep there tonight . . . Yes, in my old room . . . I don't feel like being alone either . . . What? . . . No, not yet . . . Mom, please, I'm very upset . . . I've got a lot on my mind . . . I can't decide that now . . . Mom, I don't care—lamb chops, turkey, chicken salad, anything . . .

CURTAIN

ACT III

Three weeks later.

AT RISE: B<small>UDDY</small> *has* A<small>LAN'S</small> *sports jacket in his arms, one sleeve draped over his shoulder. The jacket is putting in extra duty as* B<small>UDDY'S</small> *dancing partner.*

This is a different B<small>UDDY</small> *from the one we've seen before. In a few weeks he seems to have blossomed. He now has the assurance and self-confidence that comes with independence. He has a bounce and vitality we haven't seen before.*

He dances and chants his own rhythm.

B<small>UDDY</small>

. . . One, two, cha-cha-cha . . . Very good, cha-cha-cha . . . And turn, cha-cha-cha . . .
   (The telephone rings on "turn")
Answer phone, cha-cha-cha . . . Very good, cha-cha-cha . . .
   (He places coat on sofa saying "Excuse me, my dear." He picks up phone)
Hello? . . . Snow?
   (He sits sofa)
. . . Don't you know you could get arrested for having such a sexy voice . . . No . . . I'm still trying to get tickets for the Ionesco play that's opening tonight . . . They're supposed to call me. Then I thought we might go up to the Palladium . . . for a little . . . cha-cha-cha. Oh, say . . . could you pick me up here? It would be easier. Wonderful . . . 42 East 63rd Street. About seven? . . . Make it five to. I'm only human. Good-by.

(He hangs up, slaps his hands, and gives a little giggle of joy. Then he resumes)

Do it right, cha-cha-cha . . . Tonight's the night, cha-cha-cha . . .

(The phone rings. He picks it up. Sits on upstage end of coffee table)

Hello?

(At this moment, the door opens and ALAN enters. Or better, he drags in. This is not the ALAN of two weeks ago. He looks bedraggled. He seems to have lost a great deal of cockiness, his self-assurance. He hangs trench coat in closet and crosses downstage right to counter)

BUDDY

Yes, it is . . . Yes? . . . Oh, wonderful . . . That's two tickets for tonight . . . Yes, I'll pick them up at the box office . . . In Alan Baker's name . . . Thank you very much. Good-by.

(He hangs up. He sees ALAN)

Oh, hi, Aly. I didn't hear you come in. Gee, what a break. Your broker just got me two tickets for the Ionesco play tonight. I used your name. Is it all right?

ALAN

(Staring ahead)

Why not? I'm not using it any more.

(BUDDY gets up, picks up his dancing partner, and resumes)

BUDDY

And again, cha-cha-cha . . . To the right, cha-cha-cha . . .

(He keeps on dancing)

Where were you today?

ALAN

(Staring ahead)

At the Polo Grounds waiting for the Giants to come back . . . Anyone call?

BUDDY

(He's still dancing)

Yeah . . . a Mr. Copeland . . . and a Mr. Sampler . . . cha-cha-cha . . .

ALAN

(*Looks at him*)
What'd they say?

BUDDY

Nice and easy, cha-cha-cha . . .

ALAN

(*Angry*)
Hey, Pupi, I'm talking to you.

BUDDY

(*He stops*)
What's wrong?

ALAN

I'd like to hear one sentence without the rhythm in it. What'd
they say?

BUDDY

Who?

ALAN

(*Crossing to him*)
Copeland and Sampler, cha-cha-cha!

BUDDY

Nothing. They'll call back later. What's eating you, Alan?
(*Pats* ALAN's *shoulder and puts coat on sofa and sits*)

ALAN

It's just a little annoying to have to wait until the dance is over
to get my messages.
(*He takes coat off sofa, brushes it and hangs it in closet
upstage*)

BUDDY

Boy, you're jumpy lately. You've got a case of nerves, old boy.

ALAN

(*Crossing downstage to right center chair*)
Thank you, doctor, is my hour up?

BUDDY

What do you do all day, anyway? You're gone from ten to six.
You come home bushed. You keep getting strange calls all
day. What's all the mystery?

ALAN

There's no mystery.

BUDDY

(*Accusingly*)
Have you got a job?

ALAN

No, I haven't got a job. Are you sure no one else called?

BUDDY

You mean Connie?

ALAN

(*Expectantly*)
Connie? Why? Did she . . . ?

BUDDY

No, but you talk about her in your sleep.

ALAN

(*Sits right center chair*)
Me? You're crazy.

BUDDY

Last night you even walked in your sleep. You stretched out your arms and said, "Oh, Connie, darling" . . . I'm going to have to start locking my door.

ALAN

Are you ribbing me?

BUDDY

Why don't you call her, Alan?

ALAN

What for? I'm not interested . . . Besides . . . she checked out of her hotel.

BUDDY

Oh! Where'd she go?

ALAN

How should I know. I didn't ask them.

BUDDY

Maybe she left a forwarding address.

ALAN

There's no forwarding address.

BUDDY

How do you know?

ALAN

I asked them . . . Look, will you forget about Connie.

BUDDY

Subject closed.
  (ALAN *rises and* BUDDY *crosses to bar*)
How about a drink?

ALAN

I don't want a drink.
  (BUDDY *pours one.* ALAN *looks at him*)
What are *you* drinking for?

BUDDY

I like one at night now. Helps me unwind.
  (*Crossing right of center. He drinks*)

ALAN

What do *you* have to unwind from?

BUDDY

Oh, the little everyday problems of life.

ALAN

  (*Rises and crosses to him*)
Problems? You never had it so good. You sleep till twelve
o'clock. Lounge around until two. You go out every night.
How do you fill up the rest of the day?

BUDDY

Well, that's one of the little problems I have to unwind from.
  (ALAN *turns away right disgustedly*)
I'm just having a little fun. What's wrong, Alan?

ALAN

  (*Changing his attitude. Turns upstage*)
Nothing. Nothing, I'm sorry, kid. I don't know what's wrong
with me lately. Listen, I don't feel like sitting in again tonight. You want to go to a movie? Just the two of us?

BUDDY

  (*Puts glass on sofa table*)
Oh, gee, I'd like to, Alan, but I've got a date.

ALAN

Again? That's four times this week. Who's on tonight?

BUDDY

This one's a dancer. Modern jazz. Her name is Snow.

ALAN

Snow?

BUDDY

(*Crosses to* ALAN)
Snow Eskanazi!

ALAN

Sounds like an Italian Eskimo.

BUDDY

She's a real weirdo. Wears that white flour on her face like the Japanese Kabuki dancers. But I've got a hunch underneath she's very pretty.

ALAN

Take her out in a strong wind, maybe you'll find out . . . Where do you collect these girls, anyway?

BUDDY

I met Snow at that party I went to in the Village last Saturday.

ALAN

The one you took the Greek interpreter to?

BUDDY

Yeah. Snow was with an Indian exchange student. I was sitting on the floor next to her and she leans over and gives me her phone number. Just like that.

ALAN

How did Sabu feel about all this?

BUDDY

He loaned her the pencil. Besides, he made a date with the Greek interpreter.

ALAN

(*Sits right center chair*)
No wonder they have emergency sessions at the UN.

BUDDY

Like a jerk I went and left early. You know what I hear they
played at three o'clock in the morning?

ALAN

What?

BUDDY

Strip Scrabble!

ALAN

Strip Scrabble?? . . . I suddenly feel eighty years old. Are
you sure you're the same boy who was eating milk and cake
over a sink three weeks ago?

BUDDY

How about that, what's happened to me, Alan? You've given
me a new lease on life. Three weeks here with no one telling
me what to do and when to come home. Well, I'm a different
person, aren't I?

ALAN

Different? You're going to need identification before I let you
in here again.

BUDDY

That's why I hate to see you moping around like this.
  (*Crosses to him*)
You're a different person too. It's not like you to let yourself
go.
  (*Pats his knee*)

ALAN

  (*Indignant*)
What do you mean?

BUDDY

Well, you've been sitting home every night, you haven't called
a girl in three weeks, you're even getting to look seedy. Why
don't you call Rocco tomorrow?
  (*Crosses away left*)

ALAN

Rocco?

BUDDY

My barber.

ALAN

(*Rises and crosses to him*)

Your barber? What do you mean, *your* barber? *I* sent you
there. He's *my* barber.

BUDDY

I know. It was just a figure of speech. I didn't mean anything.
You can have him back.

(*Fixes* ALAN'S *tie*)

ALAN

I don't want him back. I just want it clear that you only go
there. But Rocco is *my* barber.

(*Turns away right, unfixes his tie*)

BUDDY

Sure, Alan, sure . . . Anyway, cheer up.

(*He pats* ALAN'S *shoulder patronizingly*)

Things'll get better.

(ALAN *sits right center chair*)

(*The doorbell rings*)

That can't be Snow. It's too early.

(*He hops over to door and opens it. It's* PEGGY *in another
crazy outfit*)

Oh, hello.

PEGGY

Hello, Mr. Manheim.

BUDDY

Come on in. You know Alan Baker.

(*He no longer fears the masquerade*)

PEGGY

Oh, sure. Hi!

(*Waves*)

I heard you were back. Is everything all right in Hollywood?

BUDDY

Oh, great. We're just about ready to roll on the picture.

PEGGY

I never got a call. I guess you found someone else for my part.

BUDDY

Not at all. We just have the male lead set. We're still looking for the girl.

PEGGY

Oh? Who did you get?

BUDDY

For what?

PEGGY

The male lead.

BUDDY

Oh. Someone new. An Italian actor.

ALAN

Rocco La Barber.

PEGGY

Oh, sure. I've heard of him.

BUDDY

Well . . . if you'll excuse me, I've got to get dressed. I've got to look over some locations tonight.

PEGGY

Of course.

BUDDY

I'll call you. I'm still very interested.
   (*Looks at his watch and shoots his cuff*)
Great Scot, it's nearly seven.
   (*Smiles at* ALAN *and prances into the bedroom*)

PEGGY

So young and so brilliant.

ALAN

Eight colleges are after his brain.

PEGGY

   (*Crosses above* ALAN)
I can understand why *he* hasn't called. What's your excuse?

ALAN

(Rises and starts left)

No excuse. I've just been busy.

PEGGY

(Stepping downstage)

And I've been lonely, Alan . . . really lonely . . .

ALAN

I haven't been doing much either.

PEGGY

(Crosses to him)

You haven't called in nearly three weeks. You never answered my messages.

ALAN

I'm sorry.

PEGGY

(Swings him around)

Prove it. Let's go to Connecticut this weekend.

ALAN

What's in Connecticut?

PEGGY

(Putting arm around him)

The ski lodge.

ALAN

It's Vermont.

PEGGY

I don't care. As long as we're together. How about it?

ALAN

(Breaking left)

Well, Peggy . . . I'm not working any more. I don't have much time for skiing.

PEGGY

(Angry. Crosses stage up right of him)

ALAN

(Stops her)

Peggy, wait. It's nothing personal. I'm still crazy about you . . . All right, look. We'll go this weekend.

PEGGY

That's more like my Alan.
(*She puts his arm around her*)
Bite me on the neck.

ALAN

What?

PEGGY

Bite me on the neck like you used to.

ALAN

Well, Peggy, I don't really feel . . .

PEGGY

Oh, come on.
(*ALAN shrugs and bites her*)

PEGGY

Ow! You bit me.
(*She breaks up to foyer, turns*)
You really *must* be a vampire.
(*She opens door and exits. ALAN crosses back down to sofa and sits*)
(*BUDDY returns wearing a sports jacket. It's one of those multicolored jobs that they advertise every Sunday in the* Times *but no one ever really buys*)

BUDDY

(*He turns around, modeling it*)
Well? How do you like the sports jacket?

ALAN

I like the lining. What's the jacket like?

BUDDY

How do you think this will go at Sardi's?

ALAN

What are you doing, going to Sardi's?

BUDDY

I thought I'd make an impression on Snow. Hey, that reminds me. I'd better make a reservation.
(*BUDDY picks up phone, and dials*)

ALAN

(*Exaggeratively swings legs on sofa out of* BUDDY'S *way*)
You certainly have blossomed into the Young Man about Town. The theater, the latest styles, Sardi's. I've created an Ivy League Frankenstein.

BUDDY

(*Into phone*)
Hello? I'd like to reserve a table for two for tonight, please. Seven-thirty . . . Oh, you are?
(*He covers phone with his hand*)
He says they're all booked up.
(*He snaps his fingers, back into phone*)
Are you sure you don't have a reservation for me? Manheim? I'm with M-G-M.
(ALAN *throws up his hands*)

BUDDY

(*Into phone*)
Yes, it was probably an oversight . . . Would you? I'd appreciate that . . . Thanks, so much. Good-by!
(*He hangs up*)
Voila!

ALAN

(*Looks up to heaven*)
What have I done?

BUDDY

(*Starts upstage and stops*)
You think he believed me?

ALAN

Why not? *I* did.

BUDDY

I'd better get moving.
(*Starts for foyer and stops and comes downstage right of* ALAN)
Oh, by the way, Alan. What are you doing about eleven-thirty tonight?

ALAN

I'll be sitting in a shawl reading the Bible. Why?

BUDDY

I hear there's a great picture at the Paris. Why don't you catch the last show. I think it lets out about one.

ALAN

I don't want to be let out about one.

BUDDY

Well, you see, I thought later on I might drop back here with Snow . . . for a nightcap.

ALAN

You what?

BUDDY

I hate to ask you, Alan, but this may be my night to conquer Mount Everest. You don't mind going to a movie, do you?

ALAN

(Rises. Seething)
You're damned right I mind!

BUDDY

What's wrong, Alan? That was our arrangement, wasn't it? If one fellow had a girl—

ALAN

That was *my* arrangement. I did the arranging and *you* went to the movies. Where do you get this *our* stuff?

BUDDY

(Quite innocently)
I thought we were splitting everything fifty-fifty?

ALAN

We were, until you got all the fifties.
(Crosses right of him and turns)
Boy, what nerve. We're not splitting anything any more. Is that understood?

BUDDY

Sure, Alan.

ALAN

Except the rent. From now on your rent is a hundred forty-two dollars a month.

BUDDY

Okay.

ALAN

(Crosses right to counter)
I think I've been bighearted long enough.

BUDDY

Alan, I never . . .

ALAN

And buy your own food too. I'm sick and tired of bringing home cookies and watching you finish them reading *my* magazines and watching *my* television.

BUDDY

You're kidding!

ALAN

(Picks up box and shakes it at him)
The hell I am. Just keep away from my Fig Newtons!

BUDDY

(Half chuckles at the ridiculousness of the situation)
I don't understand. I always give you some of my Yankee Doodles.

ALAN

(But he's not kidding. Crossing to him)
And stop eating them all over the rug with your crumbs. I never saw anything like it. Clothes lying all over the place. It's disgusting.

BUDDY

Alan, what's eating you? Is it because of this girl?

ALAN

(Crossing upstage left)
Connie? She's got nothing to do with this.

BUDDY

(Sits sofa)
Well, something's bothering you. I'd like to know what.

ALAN

Oh, you would, heh? Well, there's plenty bothering me. I happen to think you're pretty ungrateful.

BUDDY

Ungrateful!

ALAN

(*Crossing right of* BUDDY *behind sofa*)

Yes, ungrateful. I took you in here, taught you how to dress and walk and talk. Now look at you. You're a big man.

BUDDY

What's wrong, Alan? You said yourself I should grow up and become a man.

ALAN

I said become a man.

(*Points to himself*)

Not this man. Don't take my place in life.

BUDDY

How have I taken your place?

ALAN

I run the water for a bath and five minutes later I hear you splashing in there. You're using my barber, my restaurants, my ticket broker, my apartment, and my socks. How's it going, kid, am I having fun?

BUDDY

You're the one who suggested I do all these things. You said I should start having some fun.

ALAN

I said fun. Have a good time. I didn't say anything about carrying on like this.

(*Crosses right of center*)

BUDDY

Like what?

ALAN

(*Turns*)

Like a bum!

BUDDY

(*Jumps up*)
A *bum???*

ALAN

You heard me. What kind of crowd are you running around
with?
  (*Crosses to him*)
Intellectual delinquents . . . Strip Scrabble! . . . You're
lucky Interpol didn't rush in there and raid the joint.

BUDDY

What kind of girls do you know? When did that kook upstairs
get out of the Girl Scouts?

ALAN

I'm talking to *you!* Where were you until four o'clock the
other morning?

BUDDY

What's the difference?

ALAN

  (*Crosses and sits right center chair*)
I want to know where you were until four o'clock in the
morning?

BUDDY

Cocka-doodle-doo! What's with you?

ALAN

  (*Jumps up*)
Don't cocka-doodle-doo me.

BUDDY

When did you suddenly switch sides?
  (*Crosses to him*)
When I moved in here you were carrying on like every night
was New Year's Eve.

ALAN

We're not talking about a thirty-three-year-old bum. We're
talking about a twenty-one-year-old bum.

BUDDY

Oh, you mean it's all right for you.

ALAN

I mean, it's not all right for you.

(*Crosses left to coffee table*)

Three weeks ago you came in here heartsick over the fate of the world. When was the last time you picked up a newspaper or a book without a phone number in it? What happened to our young hope for a brave new world? We're losing half of South America and you're doing the cha-cha.

BUDDY

What's dancing got to do with it?

ALAN

(*Crosses to him*)

And what about looking for a job?

BUDDY

I have been.

ALAN

Since when is the employment office in an espresso joint in the Village? You're nothing but a clean-shaven beatnik.

BUDDY

I haven't asked you for anything.

ALAN

You'd have starved to death if Mom hadn't been smuggling pot-roast sandwiches through the enemy lines.

BUDDY

I didn't notice you throwing yours in the garbage can.

ALAN

At least I call her now and then. You're too busy to worry about her. And have you thought once of how Dad is getting along with the business without either of us there now?

BUDDY

What brought all this on?

ALAN

I'm seeing you for the first time.

BUDDY

You mean you're seeing yourself for the first time. I'm just a carbon copy of you.

ALAN

Well, whoever it is, I don't like it.

BUDDY

Why do *I* get the blame? You go around committing murder
and I get the chair.

ALAN

(*He raises his arm threateningly*)

Don't get smart with me. You're not too big yet to get a good
slap across the face.

BUDDY

Holy mackerel, I got two fathers!

ALAN

Cut that out. I'm nothing like him. Nothing at all.

(*Turns away left*)

BUDDY

Well, you certainly don't sound like yourself.

ALAN

(*Turns to him*)

How can I? *You're* myself now.

BUDDY

Well, maybe there's one too many of you around here.

ALAN

Maybe there is. Which one of me is leaving?

BUDDY

It's your apartment. In the meantime, I've got to shave.

(*Crosses to bedroom door and* ALAN *crosses downstage center as* BUDDY *goes up to door.* BUDDY *stops and turns*)

By the way, which is my water, the hot or the cold?

(*He stalks out of the room*)

ALAN

How do you like the nerve of that kid? Well, we'll see how
big an operator he is without me to supply him with everything.

(*Crossing left to bar and pours himself a drink. Tips glass
to his mouth and realizes there's nothing in it. He picks
up bottle and sees it's empty*)

ALAN

Connie, I'll wake up a judge tonight. I'll get down on both knees. I'll do anything, but please ... won't you marry me?

(Act III)

A whole bottle of scotch!

(*He takes empty bottle, crosses angrily to bedroom door, waves empty bottle and shouts*)

Bum!

(*He starts to bar and the doorbell rings. Puts bottle on sofa table*)

Ah, that must be Nanook of the North! . . . This I've got to see.

(*He crosses to door and opens it. The* Mother *stands there with a heavy valise*)

Mom! Mom, what are you doing here?

MOTHER

(*She trudges into the room*)

I'm lucky I'm here at all. Six blocks I had to lug this from the subway. You'd think a stranger would help a woman.

(*She puts down valise and flops in a chair*)

ALAN

(*Follows left of her*)

Mom, what are you doing with a suitcase? Where are you going?

MOTHER

I'm not going any more. I'm here.

ALAN

Here? Why?

MOTHER

For the same reason Buddy's here . . . I've run away from home.

ALAN

Mom, you're not serious?

MOTHER

Don't think I'm not ashamed. A woman of my age running away from home. I was so humiliated. A woman from my building saw me in the subway with the suitcase. I had to lie to her. I said I was going to visit my brother in California. Then at 125th Street I had to change to a local to come here.

She's not so dumb. For California you don't change at 125th Street. I should worry. My life is over anyway.

ALAN

Why, Mom? What happened?

MOTHER

What happened? Ask America what happened? In Alaska they must have heard how that man has been carrying on with me. For three weeks now. Three weeks.

ALAN

All right, Mom, he's very upset. But he'll get over it. He always does.

MOTHER

No, not this time. This time it's different. There's no making up now. I thought maybe there was a chance this morning. I was going to show him I could be bigger than he was. I wanted to show him *I* didn't forget.

ALAN

Forget what?

MOTHER

Today. It's our thirty-seventh anniversary.

ALAN

(Kneels left of her)

Oh, that's right. Happy anniversary, Mom.

(He kisses her)

MOTHER

Thank you, darling. Anyway, I went over to him. I swear to you, I had a big smile on my face, like this:

(She gives a big smile. Then goes back to her sorrow)

And then as nice as I could possibly say it, I said, "Happy Anniversary, darling. I wish you all the happiness in the world."

(She sobs)

And what do you think he said to me?

ALAN

What?

MOTHER

"Thank you . . . and I wish you what you wish me."
    (*She sobs*)
For what? What did I do he should say such a thing?

ALAN

But how do you know he meant anything wrong by that?

MOTHER

Because he knows what I was wishing him.
    (*She cries*)

ALAN

    (*Throws up his hands in futility. Crossing up right of her*)
Oh, boy!

MOTHER

All because of you two. He keeps blaming me. "Your bums.
Your two bums!"
    (BUDDY *comes out of the bedroom*)

BUDDY

    (*Crosses to left of* MOTHER; *leaves jacket on desk*)
Mom? What are you doing here?

MOTHER

    (*Crosses right to* BUDDY. *She starts right in on him*)
I'm lucky I'm here at all. Six blocks I had to lug this from the
subway.

BUDDY

Whose suitcase is that?

ALAN

My new roommate's! . . . Mom, will you listen to me.
You're just being emotional. You know you can't live here.

BUDDY

Here?

MOTHER

Where else have I got to go? A hotel? Maybe I should move
in with his sister Gussie? I'll join the Army first.

ALAN

Mom, it's not that I don't want you. But you wouldn't be
comfortable here. It's a small bachelor apartment.

MOTHER

So what am I now? I'm a bachelor too.
  (*She feels terribly sorry for herself*)
A bachelor with two grown sons.
  (*The doorbell rings*)

BUDDY

  (*Runs up to door*)
Oh, that's probably Snow.

MOTHER

You're expecting company?
  (*She picks up suitcase and starts to bedroom*)
I won't be in your way. I'll go in the bedroom with my
sewing.

ALAN

Mom, you don't have to do that.

MOTHER

You wouldn't hear me. I'll be like a dead person.

ALAN

Mom, you don't need your suitcase.

MOTHER

  (*Stopping at bedroom right door and turns*)
It's all right. I want to unpack my Alka-Seltzer. Oh, I'm so
nauseous.
  (*She holds her stomach and goes into the bedroom.*

  The doorbell rings again twice)

ALAN

  (*Crossing to counter right. To* BUDDY)
Well, answer it, lover.
  (BUDDY *crosses to door quickly and opens it. The* FATHER
  stands there, steaming)

BUDDY

Dad!

FATHER

  (*He storms in on foyer. To* BUDDY)
Where is she? I know she's here.
  (*To* ALAN)
Where's their mother?

ALAN

(*Weakly*)
In the bedroom.

FATHER

Oh, they're hiding them in the bedroom now. What's the
matter, the kitchen's being painted?
(*He crosses to bedroom and opens door. He looks in*)
Very nice. Very nice for a mother.
(BUDDY *crosses downstage and sits on sofa*)

MOTHER

(*From off stage*)
What do you want?

FATHER

What is she doing in there?

MOTHER

(*Off stage*)
She's drinking Alka-Seltzer.

FATHER

(*Crossing downstage below coffee table. Turns away*)
I thought I'd find her in here.
(*The* MOTHER *comes out with a glass in her hand. Cross-
ing downstage center*)

MOTHER

Where else should I be? They're still my children.

FATHER

She should be home. I'm still her husband.

MOTHER

Not when you treat your own children the way you do.

FATHER

This is something I will not discuss in front of strangers.

MOTHER

They're your sons.

FATHER

(*Crossing right center*)
They're *your* sons! They're my strangers! . . . Is she coming
home?

MOTHER

She's home. This is where she lives now.

FATHER

This is where she lives? With bums?

MOTHER

That's right. So that makes me a bum too. All right? Now you're happy? Now you've got three bums.

ALAN

Dad, can I say something?

FATHER

Who's he talking to? I'm not even here.

BUDDY

(*Crossing downstage left of* FATHER)

Can *I* say something?

FATHER

Write it in a play. I'll be there opening night.

ALAN

All right, Dad, please calm down. Will you talk to me for one minute?

FATHER

(*Crossing left below coffee table*)

Is she coming?

ALAN

Dad, please. It's important.

FATHER

Did the woman hear what I said?

ALAN

All right, don't answer me directly. If you understand, blink your eyes once for "yes" and twice for "no."

FATHER

(*To* MOTHER)

Did she listen to that? If I were here, I'd slap him in the mouth . . . Is she coming?

BUDDY

Dad, we can't go on like this forever.

FATHER

Forever is over. They'll have no more parents to bother them. They should be very happy.

ALAN

(Crosses left)

What do you mean, no more parents?

FATHER

(To MOTHER)

Tell him. Four months we'll be gone. I've got the tickets in my pocket.

MOTHER

You bought the tickets? I told you, I'm not going. Not until everything is all right with you and the boys.

ALAN

Going where?

FATHER

Around the world.

(Crosses right center)

Tell him around the world we're going. Ask him if that's far enough?

MOTHER

I'm not going around any worlds.

FATHER

She's going. I've got the tickets in my pocket.

ALAN

Do you mean it? Are you really going?

FATHER

(Takes ticket out of pocket and holds it up)

Here! In three weeks we'll be in China. They'll be here bumming around in peace, and we'll be in China . . . in the middle of a revolution. They'll worry a lot.

ALAN

(One step to FATHER)

But how can you leave for four months? Who's going to take care of the business?

FATHER

What business? Tell him? Is she coming around the world

. . . (*Crossing left below coffee table*) or do I take my sister Gussie?

MOTHER

I told you, I'm not going pleasure cruising with aggravation still on my heart.

ALAN

(*Crosses left to center*)
Dad, what about the business???

FATHER

Is she coming?

MOTHER

Answer him!

FATHER

I answered him. Tomorrow there'll be no business. I'm selling the business. Is that an answer?

ALAN

Selling the business?

BUDDY

Are you serious?

FATHER

Look who's suddenly so shocked. The skier and the Pulitzer Prize winner.

ALAN

(*Crossing left to him*)
Why are you selling it?

FATHER

Who should I save it for, his children?

BUDDY

But who did you sell it to, Dad?

FATHER

Who? To Chiang Kai-shek. That's why I'm going to China.
(*Crosses right to counter*)

ALAN

(*Following*)
Why, Dad. Are you selling because of us?

FATHER

You? You think I need you two? I did bigger business in the three weeks you were gone than in the six years you were there.

(*The doorbell rings*)

BUDDY

Oh, boy!

FATHER

(*To* MOTHER)

I'm not waiting any more. If she wants, I'll meet her in Hong Kong.

ALAN

Dad, wait. I've got to talk to you about this.

(*Doorbell rings*)

BUDDY

(*Looking upstage anxiously*)

Can't you talk later?

(*The doorbell rings again*)

MOTHER

Buddy, the doorbell.

BUDDY

Alan, what'll I do?

ALAN

Will you take that girl and get out of here?

(BUDDY *starts upstage*)

FATHER

(*Crossing to* BUDDY)

Girl? What girl??

BUDDY

Just a girl, Dad. Do you think you could finish this conversation in the bedroom?

FATHER

(*He can't take any more*)

The bedroom? I'll break every bone in his body.

(*He raises his arm to hit* BUDDY)

MOTHER

(*Crossing downstage left*)

Harry!

FATHER

(*Follows imitating*)

Harry, Harry.

BUDDY

(*Backing away*)

Dad, wait . . .

(*Suddenly the door opens and* CONNIE *enters*)

CONNIE

(*On foyer*)

Oh, hello!

ALAN

(*Crosses upstage to right of* CONNIE. *Stunned*)

Connie!

MOTHER

Harry, please, don't say anything.

FATHER

Don't *say* anything? No, I'll sit here and applaud.

ALAN

Connie, where have you been?

CONNIE

Cincinnati.

ALAN

Cincinnati?

CONNIE

(*Crossing downstage right to counter*)

With the Electrical Appliance Dealers of America.

(ALAN *follows her*)

FATHER

I don't have to listen to this kind of talk.

(*He starts for door left above sofa.* BUDDY *stops him*)

BUDDY

Dad, wait a minute, please.

ALAN

You mean you did another industrial show?

CONNIE

I was Miss Automatic Toaster. I popped up and sang . . .
And after the show three salesmen tried to butter me.

ALAN

But why did you take the job? You said you were quitting.

CONNIE

You changed my mind for me. Look, Alan, this doesn't seem
to be the time to discuss this . . .

ALAN

No, no. This is only my mother and father.

FATHER

Only??

CONNIE

(*Looks at her and says to* MOTHER)
Oh, hello.

MOTHER

(*Sweetly*)
How do you do?

FATHER

(*Crossing to left of her below sofa. To* MOTHER)
Are you crazy, "How do you do?"

ALAN

What do you mean, I changed your mind?

CONNIE

You were right, Alan. I'm much too talented to quit. Besides,
I'm beginning to enjoy my work.

ALAN

What work?

FATHER

What do you think, what work?
(*To* MOTHER)
You're going to stay here while this is going on?

BUDDY

(*Takes his arm*)

Dad, you don't know what you're saying.

FATHER

(*Lifts arm from shoulder exaggerating movement*)

Pushing? A father you're pushing?

MOTHER

(*Starts upstage behind sofa table*)

Harry, come in the bedroom.

CONNIE

(*Moves as if to go*)

Alan, call me later.

ALAN

(*Stops her*)

No, tell me what you're talking about.

CONNIE

Well, I really came to say good-by.

ALAN

Good-by?

CONNIE

The Electrical Dealers want me to go to Europe. With all expenses paid.

FATHER

(*Shrugs*)

She's not ashamed to say it.

CONNIE

(BUDDY *and* FATHER *exchange places*)

It's a wonderful opportunity, Alan. And after all, it's about time I had a "fling."

ALAN

A *fling*??

CONNIE

You know how it is with a twenty-four-year-old girl. She's really not ready to settle down yet.

ALAN

Connie, listen to me.
  (*The phone rings*)

FATHER

  (*Points to phone. Says to* MOTHER)
You hear? That's the cook. She'll be coming to work soon.
  (*Phone rings*)

CONNIE

I don't leave until Thursday. Call me, Alan.

BUDDY

  (*Grabs* FATHER'S *arm*)
Dad, please come inside and talk to me.

FATHER

Again he's pushing.
  (*The phone keeps ringing*)

ALAN

Connie, you can't go to Europe. I won't let you.
  (*Phone rings*)

MOTHER

Alan, your phone.

CONNIE

You won't *let* me?

ALAN

Connie, I need you.
  (*Phone rings*)
I didn't realize it until you were out of my life for three weeks.
I couldn't stand it. I love (*phone rings*) you, sweetheart.

MOTHER

  (*Crosses to right of center*)
Alan, your phone.

CONNIE

Alan, we've been through those words before.

ALAN

I didn't really feel (*phone rings*) this way before. You've got
to believe me. It's all over. I have flung!
  (*Ring*)

MOTHER
(Crosses left to coffee table)
Buddy, the phone.

BUDDY
Dad . . .

FATHER
(To BUDDY)
If he pushes me once more, he'll bleed from the nose.

BUDDY
I wasn't pushing you.
(The phone rings)

MOTHER
Maybe I'm crazy. No one hears a phone.
(She picks it up)

CONNIE
Alan, are you sure?

MOTHER
(Into phone)
Hello?

CONNIE
Are you really sure?

ALAN
I was never so sure of anything in my life.

MOTHER
Alan, it's for you.

ALAN
I'm busy, Mom. Take a message.

MOTHER
Again with a message.

BUDDY
Who is it, Mom?

MOTHER
Do I know? Do I have a pencil?

BUDDY
All right, don't get excited.

FATHER

That's right. Yell at your mother. Push *her!*

BUDDY

(*Crosses upstage above sofa table*)

I wasn't pushing!

MOTHER

Alan, it's a Mr. Kaplan or Koplon . . . Oh, I'm so nauseous.

FATHER

Copeland? From Begley's Department Store in Texas? . . .
Give me that.

(*He grabs phone*)

ALAN

(*Crossing left*)

No, Dad—

FATHER

(*Into phone*)

Hello? . . . Mr. Copeland of Texas? . . . How do you do,
sir . . . To what do I owe the honor of this phone call? . . .
Order? What order? . . . Yes, of course it's Mr. Baker . . .
No, his father . . . Oh . . . just a minute.

(*He is bewildered. He looks front but hands him phone*)

It's for him.

ALAN

(*Into phone*)

Hello, Mr. Copeland . . . You what? . . . Oh, wonderful
. . . The same order we talked about today? . . . Yes, I've
got it. You'll have the shipment the first of the month . . .
Not at all . . . Have a nice trip back . . . and thank you . . .
Good-by.

(*He hangs up*)

FATHER

(*Stares at him*)

How does he come to know Copeland of Texas?

ALAN

I heard he was in town. I called him and took him out to
lunch a few times . . . alone.

(*He takes out paper from his pocket*)
I guess *you'd* better take care of this order, Dad.
    (FATHER *takes paper and looks at it in disbelief*)

FATHER

Four years I'm after Copeland of Texas.

BUDDY
   (*Crosses downstage right of* ALAN)
So that's what you've been doing every day. Working. And
all those phone calls from Copeland and Sampler.

FATHER

Sampler too? . . . I just got a telegram for a big order tonight.
For transparent grapes.

ALAN

I thought I owed you that much, Dad.

FATHER
  (*To* ALAN)
Owed me?
  (*Then crosses left*)
He owes me nothing. I don't need his orders.
  (*Puts invoice in pocket*)

ALAN
  (*Crosses left to him*)
Dad, please. Even if you don't want me to work for you, can't
we at least be friends?

FATHER
  (*Angry. Away from* ALAN)
I don't need a bum for a friend.

ALAN

Why am I bum?

FATHER

Is he married?

ALAN

Yes!

FATHER

Then he's a bu—
  (*He stops short and turns to* ALAN)
What????

ALAN

That is . . . I will be if Connie says yes.

(He crosses right to CONNIE *who steps to him)*

Connie, I'll wake up a judge tonight. I'll get down on both knees. I'll do anything, but please . . . won't you marry me?

CONNIE

Oh, darling.

(They kiss)

*(*CONNIE *nudges him)*

ALAN

Huh!

(Turns to others)

Mom, I guess you can call the caterers . . . This is Connie Dayton. The girl I'm going to marry.

BUDDY

No kidding?

*(*CONNIE *crosses left to* MOTHER. *They meet right center)*

MOTHER

Oh, darling.

(She and CONNIE *embrace)*

BUDDY

(Crosses to MOTHER*)*

Gee, congratulations.

(They all look at ALAN *who then looks for approval from the* FATHER. *They all turn and look at* FATHER*)*

ALAN

Dad—

(The FATHER *turns away from them)*

MOTHER

Harry, your son is going to get married.

FATHER

No one tells me nothing. All I get is pushed.

ALAN

(Crosses left to FATHER*)*

Dad, I don't know how to say this to you . . . but . . . well, you were right about so many things.

(FATHER *nods . . . huh . . . huh*)

I was a bum.

(FATHER *nods . . . huh . . . huh*)

I guess every boy's got to be a bum even for a little while. I just ran into overtime.

(FATHER *nods . . . huh . . . huh*)

There's a lot more I want to say to you, Dad, but not now. Look, why don't we all go out to celebrate? To a night club.

(*Crosses right to* CONNIE)

FATHER

He hasn't got a job, he's going to night clubs.

MOTHER

Harry, the children want to take us out.

FATHER

Let them save their money for furniture.

ALAN

(*Afraid things are going to start all over again*)

Oh, Dad, can't you just once—

CONNIE

No, Alan, Alan.

(*Leaping into the breach. Crosses left to* FATHER)

Mr. Baker is right. It's impossible to talk in night clubs any-way. And tonight I'd like to talk. After all, I suddenly have a new family.

(*To* MR. BAKER, *tenderly*)

Please Mr. Baker . . . why don't we all have dinner together.

FATHER

(*He turns slowly to see who this girl is. She looks "nice." "Very nice." And suddenly he has no more sons. Now he's got a daughter. He smiles. Removes hat and places it over his heart and bows*)

Well . . . Maybe just for a cup of coffee.

ALAN

(*Crosses left to* CONNIE)

Thanks, Dad.

FATHER

(*To* ALAN . . . *warning*)

But we come home early. You've got to be at the plant eight o'clock in the morning and I don't want any excuses.

ALAN

Do you mean that? Do you really want me back?

FATHER

No, I'm going to put the night watchman in charge while I'm in China.

ALAN

(*Laughs—starts upstage taking* CONNIE)

Come on, everybody.

CONNIE

(*On way up stops at* BUDDY)

Good night, Buddy.

(*She kisses him and continues to foyer*)

BUDDY

Good night, Connie.

MOTHER

(*Crosses to* BUDDY)

Buddy, darling, you do whatever you want, sweetheart. You're not a baby any more.

BUDDY

Thanks, Mom.

(*He kisses her*)

MOTHER

But be up for dinner Friday night.

BUDDY

I will.

MOTHER

And bring your laundry.

(*Crosses to bedroom to get valise and coat*)

BUDDY

(*As* FATHER *starts toward door*)

Well, Dad, you still haven't said anything. Is it OK to leave home?

FATHER

(*Stops*)

No.

BUDDY

Oh, Dad.

FATHER

(*Crosses to* BUDDY)

So what are you asking me?

(ALAN *crosses left of* FATHER *behind sofa*)

If I say "no" it's "yes" anyway. There was a time when my "no" was "no," but now you're twenty-one and "no" is "yes." So it's "yes" and forget the "no."

(ALAN *and* BUDDY *exchange puzzled looks*)

(*He takes valise from* MOTHER *who has come out of bedroom and they all start out*)

BUDDY

(*As* FATHER *goes off*)

Thanks, Dad.

ALAN

(*Has put on coat*)

See you back here later? . . . About twelve?

BUDDY

Make it one.

ALAN

(*Smiles*)

Right, Mr. Manheim.

(*He goes to door and turns*)

So long . . . bum!

(*He exits*)

(BUDDY *looks after him, crosses to upstage left desk and gets jacket. Puts jacket on and looks around room. He crosses now to sofa and arranges pillows. Doorbell rings.* BUDDY *crosses to downstage left lamp and turns it out*)

BUDDY

Coming, my Snowflake!

(*He goes to door, composes himself, then opens it. A* WOMAN *in her fifties stands there*)

Aunt Gussie!

(*Curtain starts down*)

WOMAN

(*She walks into room as curtain falls*)

I was in the neighborhood, so I thought I'd say hello.

CURTAIN